THE CHINESE CIVIL SERVICE

Career Open to Talent?

11/66

PROBLEMS IN ASIAN CIVILIZATIONS

THE CHINESE CIVIL SERVICE

Career Open to Talent?

EDITED WITH AN INTRODUCTION BY

Johanna M. Menzel

COLUMBIA UNIVERSITY

D. C. HEATH AND COMPANY · BOSTON

Table of Contents

Introduction

When the right men are available, government flourishes.
When the right men are not available, government declines.

THESE words from the Doctrine of the Mean, one of the Confucian classics, have been echoed by generations of Chinese statesmen under the empire. Whether coping with routine problems of administration or facing serious crises in the life of the state, political thinkers and practical men of affairs alike were agreed that the recruitment of men of talent into the service of the state was the chief remedy for any problem at hand. Legal and institutional change, so much pursued in the Western political tradition as a remedy for political ailments, has had to take second place in the Chinese tradition behind the search for "men of talent."

The idea that the ruler should be served by a group of advisers preeminent for their moral integrity and wisdom has deep roots in Chinese history. It probably derives from Confucius' insistence that the essence of righteous rule is moral guidance, and it was transmitted to the men of the early empire in the writings of the Confucian school. When the Han dynasty (206 B.C.–221 A.D.) began to reorganize the centralized, bureaucratic empire of the Ch'in (221–206 B.C.), these Confucian ideas began to affect public policy. The first steps were taken to organize the recruitment of civil servants on the basis of merit; appointments to official posts went to "men of talent" who had been recommended to the capital on the initiative of local officials. Later on, examinations were used to supplement recommendation as a measure of talent. It was during the Han dynasty, too, that the earliest link between an official career and an education in the Confucian classics was established when the government began to employ the Confucian-trained graduates of the National University.

After several centuries of division, the Sui (589–618) and T'ang (618–906) dynasties saw in the training and recruitment of a centralized civil service the best means of overcoming the powers of regionalism and of the hereditary aristocracy. To train such an elite of merit, the T'ang organized a regular system of examinations and began to recruit a substantial number of its officials from among examination graduates. The subsequent major Chinese dynasties, the Sung (960–1279) and Ming (1368–1644) as well as the sinicized Manchus (1644–1912) relied heavily on a series of public, competitive examinations to recruit state officials. By Ming times, examinations at three levels—prefectural, provincial, and metropolitan—led to three successive degrees which have often (though erroneously) been identified with the Western sequence of Bachelor, Master, and Doctor. (A glossary of Chinese degree and examination terms is included at the end of this introduction.) For the most part, only a degree qualified a man for service in officialdom.

During earlier dynasties, there had been much experimentation with the contents of the examinations. During the T'ang dynasty, for instance, degrees were offered in any one of several fields, including classics, letters, law, and others. By Ming times, this range had narrowed considerably; examinations had become standardized and consisted chiefly of the Confucian classics in their orthodox interpretation, defined by the Sung philosopher Chu Hsi.

Refined by the changing experiences and tastes of successive generations, the examination system developed into one of the chief ornaments of the traditional Chinese state. Within the government, questions concerning the civil service, its recruitment and composition, and the examination system and its adequacy, were among the most closely studied and bitterly contested issues. The periodic examinations meanwhile became the great public events of Chinese political life. The impecunious scholar, on his way to the capital to take part in the examinations, became a stock figure in Chinese fiction and drama as early as the Sung dynasty.

By Sung times, too, the scholar-official had become clearly established at the pinnacle of the Chinese social structure; his career, like no other in China or elsewhere, gave a man simultaneous access to power, prestige, and wealth. The rise of this aristocracy of merit had by now definitely freed the dynasty from its dependence on an older, hereditary aristocracy. Some historians have considered the rise of this new elite, variously called "gentry" or "scholar-officials," important enough to make it the beginning of modern Chinese history.

The regular use of examinations to recruit officialdom had lasting consequences for culture as well as for society. The traditions of Chinese thought and learning began to be shaped increasingly by the standards and practices of the examination system. The arduous and time-consuming preparations for the examination made aspirants for office lead a virtual "examination life," which may have stifled originality and bred conformity. At any rate, it drew the intellectual energies of generations of Chinese into the orbit of the state.

Western observers had early identified the civil service as one of the unique marks of the Chinese body politic. Matteo Ricci, architect and early chronicler of the Jesuit mission to China, gave a detailed and admiring description of the contents and procedure of the examination system. Later in the seventeenth century and particularly in the eighteenth, reports about the civil service recruited on the basis of virtue drew the warm admiration of the *philosophes*. Voltaire, Turgot, and many others in their writings helped to fix the image of the Chinese civil service as a career open to talent, and used such information as they possessed to attack the forces of privilege and heredity in the Europe of their day. It was not the first nor the last time that a half-truth about China enlivened Western political argument.

The serious study of the examination system and the degree to which it provided a "career open to talent" began only around the turn of the twentieth century. By now, Western scholars had a more mature historical tradition as well as the resources of several of the newer social sciences to bring to bear on the examination of Chinese data. At the same time, the West's earlier admiration for things Chinese had given place to a more sober appraisal, even to the tendency to "debunk" the previously much admired Chinese state and its institutions. By the turn of the century, Chinese scholars too were beginning to gain a new perspective on the institutions of their traditional state. The abolition of the examination system in 1905 and of the empire seven years later gave them a new freedom to subject traditional institutions to close criticism. The seepage of Western thought into China, specially in the 1910's and 1920's, furnished new ideological positions from which to judge the adequacy of traditional procedures.

In this more critical frame of mind, Chinese and Western scholars began to inquire whether the civil service examinations had in fact brought as much new blood into officialdom as had been claimed. The earliest attempt to measure quantitatively the amount of mobility into the civil service was undertaken at the very end of the nineteenth century. In a pioneer study, Father

Étienne Zi examined the social and ethnic backgrounds and subsequent careers of some three hundred men who had earned the highest degree, the *chin-shih*, with distinction. He also investigated the educational and social backgrounds of the empire's highest office-holders and found that while Chinese outnumbered Manchus among the most distinguished degree holders, Manchus outnumbered Chinese in the highest civil service posts. Ethnic background—i.e., being a Manchu—Father Zi concluded, provided a much surer basis for entry into the highest ranks of officialdom than did intellectual or moral excellence as measured by examination.[1]

While Father Zi's data reflected the special characteristics of officialdom under a "dynasty of conquest," the more general question he posed has challenged historians and social scientists to this day. They have examined social mobility, and particularly mobility into the civil service, for all the major dynasties in the last thousand years. Like Father Zi, later scholars have examined the social backgrounds and careers of Chinese degree holders and office-holders to discover whether the civil service in fact recruited "men of talent" regardless of social background or whether it was, after all, dominated by a relatively small group of "great families" who exercised power over long stretches of time. Some of the most important studies of the subject are reproduced in the first section of this volume.

The earliest dynasty for which adequate data are available, the Sung, has been investigated by Professor E. A. Kracke, Jr., (pages 1–8). Professor Kracke's pointed formulation of the issue, "Family vs. Merit in the Chinese Civil Service Examinations," has also been used by Professor Ping-ti Ho in his study of Ming and Ch'ing officialdom (pages 28–33). Both scholars examine the social backgrounds of successful *chin-shih* to determine how many graduates have

emerged from previously commoner, non-office-holding families and how many from already office-holding families. It is the high percentage of *commoners* recruited into officialdom through the examination system, Professors Kracke and Ho believe, which is the true measure of mobility in traditional China.

Other scholars have been more concerned with other aspects of the graduates' social background. Professors P'an Kuang-tan and Fei Hsiao-t'ung, for example, are interested in the relative inequality of opportunity which made it much easier for city-bred candidates than for country-dwellers to pass the civil service examinations (pages 9–21). They suspect, but do not systematically explore, that wealth, especially landed wealth, must be available to a commoner family before one of its members can acquire the education that promises success in the examinations.

When presenting themselves for examination, the Chinese candidates were required to supply information on degrees and offices held by their paternal forebears as well as on their places of residence. It is these data which have enabled Professors Kracke, Ho, P'an, and Fei to study the social backgrounds of examination candidates. Information on the candidate's financial status or the wealth of his family, however, was not required; the study of wealth as a factor in mobility is, therefore, severely handicapped. We may never know whether it was wealth or talent which permitted certain commoners' sons to ascend into officialdom. Some insight into the role of wealth in the recruitment process is nevertheless furnished by Professor Chang Chung-li (pages 22–27). Professor Chang demonstrates that in certain periods of Chinese history when the government sold degrees or offices for money, wealth could be directly transformed into official rank. Even for those who sought office by the regular path of examination, not purchase, wealth could play a key role: it alone could provide the leisure for the prolonged course of studies

[1] See the "Suggestions for Additional Reading" at the end of the book for exact bibliographic reference.

which preceded the examinations; it could hire tutors and, in exceptional cases, bribe examination officials.

Many of these empirical studies do not measure entrance into officialdom directly; instead, they measure entry into the broader group of degree holders from among whom officials were selected. It is probably true that at all times the degree holders were more numerous than the official positions. In fact, only the highest degree, the *chin-shih,* was meant to lead a man almost automatically to official appointment. A person holding the intermediate, or *chü-jen,* degree might be employed in the lower ranks of officialdom, but had no guarantee of such employment. The lowest degree holder, *sheng-yüan,* was virtually never employed on the basis of degree alone. Entry into officialdom and entry into the group of degree holders were thus by no means the same thing. Still, there is some relationship between the two processes, since degree-holding was usually a prerequisite for appointment to office. Moreover, even the lower degree holders who lacked official posts were at times entrusted with quasi-governmental functions. The student should pay close attention in each case to the nature of the group whose social origins are being examined.

The examination of degree holders and their social backgrounds is a useful approach to our subject because during the last thousand years of the traditional Chinese state, examination and degree-holding had become the royal road to office. Other paths to office nevertheless existed, or could be used as shortcuts to office in combination with examination. Several scholars have therefore systematically explored such alternative or supplementary paths to office to get a more rounded picture of social mobility in China.

Our chief example of such an approach is the selection from Professor Karl A. Wittfogel (pages 34–40). Professor Wittfogel examines the hereditary (*yin*) privilege which permitted the entrance of officials' sons into officialdom without exami-

nation. Widespread use of this privilege does not necessarily imply that the men so recruited lacked talent; on the contrary, as the advocates of the hereditary privilege pointed out, officials' sons had the opportunity to absorb in the home many of the skills and points of view which qualified a man for assumption of office. Nevertheless, were we to find extensive use of the hereditary privilege in the recruitment of civil servants, it would confirm the view of the Chinese civil service as essentially the preserve of a minority of important families.

Professor Wittfogel's view that the hereditary privilege indeed contributed to the monopoly of a few great families over the civil service is challenged in a study by Francis L. K. Hsü (pages 41–48). In a study of downward mobility, Professor Hsü finds that the inability of once prominent families to maintain prominence over several generations disproves the view of the civil service as essentially the preserve of a few self-perpetuating houses.

Studies of Chinese elite mobility have been carried on in the context of a debate about the nature of China's traditional society. Stimulated or repelled by Marxist attempts at "class analysis," scholars have for several decades grappled with the problem of social stratification in traditional China. Needless to say, the studies on social mobility reproduced in this volume reflect some of the emphases and semantic difficulties of the debate on social stratification. The student is referred to the bibliographical essay for some pertinent literature, and should meanwhile note carefully that the authors here represented have used such crucial terms as "elite," "gentry," and "commoners" in rather diverse ways.

While most studies to date have been concerned with *recruitment into* the civil service, recently the patterns of *promotion within* officialdom have also been studied. The old question of family vs. merit reappears in a new form: did non-bureaucratic considerations (family background, wealth, etc.) determine an official's promotion, or was promotion chiefly determined by bureaucratic criteria such as merit or seniority? For the Ch'ing dynasty, the problem has been examined by Robert M. Marsh (pages 49–56).

The study of recruitment and promotion in the civil service had begun primarily as an exercise in *social history,* as a study of the amounts and patterns of social mobility. In the meantime, it has become clear that such investigations have much to contribute to an understanding of China's *political history* and that, in fact, patterns of mobility cannot be wholly understood outside their political context. The interpretations which emphasize this political context are reproduced in the second section of this volume.

The chief impetus toward this view of the problem has come from certain pioneers who have boldly generalized and speculated about the nature of the Chinese state. In our century, Max Weber has called attention to the close relationship between the emergence of a civil service recruited on a merit basis and the demise of feudalism in China; similarly, he sees a connection between the high rate of mobility into and out of the civil service on the one hand, and the failure of the officials to form a countervailing force against the dynasty's absolutism, on the other. His views are presented on pages 57–60. In its most pointed form, Weber's argument has recently been revived by Professor Wittfogel in his study of *Oriental Despotism.* So far from creating an "open society," high social mobility in this view becomes the basis of a despotic imperial regime (pages 61–66).

Among other studies of the political aspect of recruitment, Professor Kracke's article (pages 67–75) shows how the manipulation of regional quotas in the examination system was used by the dynasty to achieve desired political ends. Professor Heinz Friese's contribution proves that recruitment procedures for entry into the civil service came to be intimately involved in the power struggle of factions at court (pages 77–83). Other students of the examination system have shown that important changes in recruitment procedures and hence in mobility may coincide with major political crises in the lives of dynasties, and they are beginning to suspect that there is some as yet unexplored relationship between recruitment procedure, effective mobility, and the dynastic cycle.

In recent years, the recruitment procedures of the civil service have been studied in yet another context: that of the history of ideas and values. The interpretations which reflect this interest have been collected in the third and last section of this volume. The question now has shifted away from the social background and political context of officialdom. Instead, historians have begun to ask questions about the concept of "talent" and the nature of the education which qualified a man for office in traditional China.

Some recent arguments have followed a line that was first expressed by Matteo Ricci in the seventeenth century. In one of his most incisive observations, the great Jesuit remarked:

It is evident to everyone here that no one will labor to attain proficiency in mathematics or in medicine who has any hope of becoming prominent in the field of philosophy. The result is that scarcely anyone devotes himself to these studies unless he is deterred from the pursuit of what are considered to be the higher studies, either by reason of family affairs or by mediocrity of talent. The study of mathematics and that of medicine are held in low esteem, because they are not fostered by honors as is the study of philosophy, to which students are attracted by the hope of glory and the rewards attached to it. This may be readily seen in the interest taken in the study of moral philosophy. The man who is promoted to the higher degrees in this field, prides himself on the fact that he has in truth attained to the pinnacle of Chinese happiness.[2]

[2] *China in the Sixteenth Century: The Journals of Matthew Ricci, 1583–1610,* tr. Louis J. Gallagher, S.J., Random House, New York, 1942, pp. 32–33.

From the last third of the nineteenth century on, some Chinese recognized that China's backwardness in technology was due in part to the educational and intellectual traditions which had been fostered and perpetuated by the examination system, based as it was on the study of philosophical, literary, and historical classics in the Confucian tradition to the exclusion of science and technology. But the status of the higher technician in the service of the state had become a live issue centuries before the "self-strengtheners" of the late nineteenth century had to raise it anew.

Discussing the status of craftsmen and technicians in the Ming civil service (pages 77–83), Professor Heinz Friese reveals much about the educational ideals of that time, particularly a kind of hierarchy of qualifications in which character, intellectual ability, and technical skill ranked in sharply descending order.

Much remains obscure about the way in which the Chinese of the Ming or any other dynasty conceived the relationship of character and ability. Yet that relationship was crucial to the working of the civil service and its recruitment procedures. "Character" and "integrity," everyone agreed, were the true mark of the qualified official. Yet, in practice, ability was often substituted as a measure of the man, and it was, in any case, easier to measure than character. One attempt to supplement the examination of ability with a personal and responsible appraisal of a man's character is reported in Professor Kracke's study of sponsorship under the Sung dynasty (pages 84–91). Yet if the Sung dynasty succeeded temporarily in a balanced assessment of character *and* intellectual ability, the tendency was in most dynasties to base recruitment on the measurable, quantifiable attributes of human intelligence, memory, and even penmanship (as revealed in the civil service examinations) in place of the more intangible moral stature of a man. It was this very substitution of tangible but secondary criteria in place of the intangible which provoked much criticism of the Chinese examination system through the cen-

turies. This criticism, detailed in the article by Professor Nivison (pages 92–106), makes clear that to the Chinese, the issue was more serious than the perennial American question of objective vs. subjective course examinations in the schools. The Chinese were in fact groping for some outward sign of an inner grace that qualified a man for political leadership. To study the recruitment procedures of the Chinese civil service, therefore, is to observe the interplay of ideas and institutions in one very crucial area of Chinese experience.

The readings brought together in this book do not always form a debate. More often, they are in the nature of a progressive exploration of a many-sided and complex subject. For this reason, I have felt free to include more than one contribution from an author where its quality and subject matter seemed appropriate. To have done so in a "debate" might have swung the balance of views unfairly in one direction; not to have done so here would have deprived this book of some of its better ingredients.

Because the authors do at times take issue with each other, I have reproduced their footnotes where they seemed to clarify the argument. But I have used my discretion and have left out many explanatory notes and all notes which merely cited bibliographical references.

In contrast to many scholars in Western history, the contributors to this book are not even sure of an agreed body of fact over whose interpretation they differ. Indeed, they are only slowly becoming aware of the dimensions of their subject. Yet if the scholarly tradition is still young, it shows promise of fruitful cooperation across disciplinary lines. Since historians and social scientists have together explored the Chinese civil service, this distillation of their findings and approaches will, I hope, attract not only the student of Chinese history proper but all historians and social scientists with an interest in the comparative study of societies.

GLOSSARY OF CHINESE TERMS*

STATE EXAMINATIONS

T'ung-shih
An entrance examination, in three parts, given at the district and prefectural levels, leading to the *sheng-yüan* degree.

Yu-kung
A triennial examination given to highly qualified *sheng-yüan* and leading to the *kung-sheng* degree.

Pa-kung
An examination held every twelve years, given to highly qualified *sheng-yüan* and leading to the *kung-sheng* degree.

Hsiang-shih
A triennial provincial examination open to qualified *sheng-yüan, chien-sheng,* and *kung-sheng* and leading to the *chü-jen* degree.

Hui-shih
A triennial metropolitan examination open to *chü-jen* and leading to the *kung-shih* degree.

Tien-shih
A triennial palace examination, held immediately after the preceding *hui-shih* examination. It led to the *chin-shih* degree and served to rank the *chin-shih* in order of distinction.

DEGREES

Sheng-yüan
"Government Student," or "Bachelor" in some Western works; there were various subgroups, some of which were on government stipends. Degree holders had to undergo frequent further examinations to retain *sheng-yüan* status and qualify for higher examination. *Sheng-yüan* were not eligble for government posts. Most authors include them in the "gentry" or "elite."

Hsiu-ts'ai
"Budding Talent," a popular name for *sheng-yüan.*

Chien-sheng
"Student of the Imperial College," but not necessarily in attendance. The degree could be acquired by purchase, imperial favor, or inheritance; the holder was not eligible for office, but was qualified to participate in the examination for the *chü-jen* degree either in his native province or in the capital district where a special quota existed.

Kung-sheng
"Imperial Student"; degree acquired through examination ("regular *kung-sheng*") or purchase ("irregular *kung-sheng*"). The holder was eligible for office and for the *hsiang-shih* examination in his home province or the capital district.

Chü-jen
"Recommended Man," or "Master" in some Western works. The degree was not for sale; the holder was eligible for office.

Kung-shih
"Presented Scholar," graduate of the triennial metropolitan examination. Usually the holder advanced automatically to the next degree.

Chin-shih
"Metropolitan Graduate," or "Doctor" in some Western works. The highest degree and usually led to office. Note: During the Sung dynasty, there existed no degree below *chin-shih.*

Ming-ching
"Doctor in Classics," a degree in use during the T'ang dynasty when it contrasted with the *chin-shih,* or "Doctor in Letters."

* Terms and definitions are based largely on Professor Chang Chung-li's *The Chinese Gentry* and reflect conditions that prevailed in Ch'ing times. Articles dealing with earlier dynasties usually explain in which way the earlier degree structure differed from the later, better-known system.

MAJOR CHINESE DYNASTIES*

PERIOD	NATIVE	FOREIGN	PERIOD
206 B.C.–221 A.D.	Han		
589–618	Sui		
618–906	T'ang		
960–1279	Sung	Liao	947–1125
		Chin	1122–1234
		Yüan	1271–1368
1368–1644	Ming		
		Ch'ing	1644–1912

* The overlapping of major dynasties usually means that a foreign "dynasty of conquest" was already established in north China while a native dynasty still held sway in the south.

The Conflict of Opinion

THE CHINESE CIVIL SERVICE AND SOCIAL MOBILITY

"A considerable accession to the civil service of men without official background was made possible by the examinations. . . . Graduates who had no family tradition of civil service played, by virtue both of their numbers and of their official functions, a highly significant part."

—E. A. KRACKE, JR.

"The examination system was not completely monopolized by the families already holding degrees, but at the same time, the opportunity for upward social mobility provided by the examination system was not too great. . . . The opportunity for residents of the countryside . . . was not as great as for urban residents."

—P'AN KUANG-TAN AND FEI HSIAO-T'UNG

"The examination system did indeed make possible a certain 'equality of opportunity,' but the advantages were heavily in favor of those who had wealth and influence."

CHANG CHUNG-LI

"Modern students without preconceived theories or prejudice would perhaps rather agree with François Quesnay, a typical eighteenth-century French *philosophe,* who . . . believed with basically valid reason that by and large the Chinese ruling class was recruited on the basis of individual merit."

—PING-TI HO

"The Sui and T'ang dynasties which established and elaborated the world's greatest system of competitive examinations were careful to insure access to office to the direct descendants of the acting bureaucracy without examination. . . . The [hereditary] privilege must be seen as a specific aspect of the Chinese examination system not only in such essentially Chinese dynasties as T'ang, Sung and Ming, but also in the great periods of conquest, Liao, Chin, Yüan and Ch'ing."

—KARL A. WITTFOGEL

"The hereditary privilege notwithstanding, there is substantial evidence in support of the view that a fairly high degree of social mobility existed in Chinese society during the last thousand years."

—FRANCIS L. K. HSÜ

"In the Ch'ing bureaucracy the rule of seniority and other norms operated in such a way as to equalize the chances for advancement of officials from family backgrounds as disparate in privilege as official families and commoner families.

—ROBERT M. MARSH

RECRUITMENT AND THE STRUGGLE FOR POWER

"From the emperor's standpoint, the examination system . . . facilitated a competitive struggle for prebends and offices among the candidates, which stopped them from joining together into a feudal office nobility. Admittance to the ranks of aspirants was open to everybody who was proved to be educationally qualified. The examination system thus fulfilled its purpose."

—MAX WEBER

"The examinations provided the ambitious core of the ruling class with a most intensive intellectual and doctrinal training; and they added a varying amount of 'fresh blood' to the ranking officialdom. But they did not destroy the trend toward socio-political self-perpetuation which dominated the thoughts and actions of this group."

—KARL A. WITTFOGEL

"In the course of centuries the dominant trend of Chinese opinion has continued for the most part to recognize the need for equal opportunity in the examinations. In defining the desirable form of 'equal opportunity,' however, political conditions of different periods have led to shifting formulations, which have stressed variously equality for the individual, the racial group, or the region."

—E. A. KRACKE, JR.

THE ATTEMPT TO MEASURE TALENT

"The key question really was whether achievement in any field—except the military—without moral qualification entitled a man to a post in officialdom. The answer clearly was no.

—HEINZ FRIESE

"The method of competitive examination offered a way of testing abstract reasoning powers and skills that could be formally taught, but it could not foretell how a man would meet the practical challenges that faced an official. . . . Sponsorship seemed particularly suited to supply the deficiencies of the examination method."

—E. A. KRACKE, JR.

"For all the attention scholars have given to the imperial examination system and its ramifications, the long tradition of protest against the system has been almost completely ignored. . . . The complaint that the examinations failed to nourish talents of practical use to the state was not a new and radical idea in the nineteenth century; on the contrary, it was a familiar criticism in the ninth."

—DAVID S. NIVISON

THE CHINESE CIVIL SERVICE
AND SOCIAL MOBILITY

Family vs. Merit in the Examination System

E. A. KRACKE, JR.

E. A. Kracke, Jr., Professor of Chinese History at the University of Chicago, is one of the foremost students of the Sung period and a specialist on the Chinese civil service. From among his several contributions to our subject, three are reproduced in this book. In this selection, Professor Kracke defined the terms of the debate as they were to be understood for some time to come: Did the Chinese examination system recruit men of talent regardless of their social, political, or ethnic backgrounds? While the question was not new in 1947, Professor Kracke here used a new kind of evidence to give an answer for the Sung period.

1. THE PROBLEM: DID THE CIVIL SERVICE EXAMINATIONS INTRODUCE NEW BLOOD INTO THE CHINESE CIVIL SERVICE?

One of China's most significant contributions to the world has been the creation of her system of civil service administration, and of the examinations which from 622 to 1905 served as the core of that system. While these inventions have inspired the development of our civil service systems in the West, recent writers have denied that the examinations fulfilled their avowed function in their native land itself.

Did the civil service examinations of China's traditional governmental system— the "Confucian state"—permit the free rise of talent from non-bureaucratic families to positions of governmental responsibility? Or on the contrary did the body of public officials form a distinct, exclusive, hereditary bureaucratic class? Was the professed intention to seek ability wherever it could be found an elaborate hoax, on most Chinese as well as on the rest of the world? The importance of the problem is clear. Its answer will influence basically our conception of the Chinese state and Chinese society from 200 B.C. to 1911 A.D. It will also affect our understanding of the social and political role of Confucianism, which sponsored the examination system.

Western answers to the questions involved have swung between two extremes. The early European idealization of the examinations is reflected by Quesnay, writing in 1767:

There is no hereditary nobility in China; a man's merit and capacity alone mark the rank he is to take. Children of the prime minister of the empire have their fortune to make and enjoy no special consideration . . . To succeed him in his dignities

From E. A. Kracke, Jr., "Family vs. Merit in the Chinese Civil Service Examinations During the Empire," *Harvard Journal of Asiatic Studies*, X (1947), pp. 103–05, 108–123. Reprinted by permission.

1

and to enjoy his reputation, the son must elevate himself by the same steps; thus all of the son's hopes depend on study, as the only avenue to honors.

Today, on the other hand, the democratic aspect of the examination system is often discounted. The ground for the view now widely accepted was outlined by Dr. K. A. Wittfogel in 1938, when he announced certain preliminary results of his survey of source materials on China's social and economic structure. To obtain some quantitative evidence on the social position of fathers and grandfathers of the average Chinese official, particularly in the period 618-1911, research workers under his direction checked data in a number of biographic collections of the Han, Chin, T'ang, Sung, Yüan, Ming and Ch'ing dynasties. It was stated that these biographies were mostly, except for the Ch'ing, taken from the dynastic histories. On the basis of this material, Dr. Wittfogel reached the preliminary conclusion that

Some "fresh blood" may have been absorbed from the lower strata of society by means of the examination system; but on the whole the ruling officialdom reproduced itself socially more or less from its own ranks. The Chinese system of examinations had a very definite function; but . . . this function is by no means what popular legend has thus far made us believe it was.

This evidence drawn from biographic sources is in sharp contrast with that afforded by a source hitherto ignored—the earliest lists of civil service examination graduates which remain to us in substantially complete form. These lists, dated 1148 and 1256, present the names of the successful candidates for the *chin-shih* degree in the order of their examination grades. They also supply, along with other biographical and academic details, information on the official careers of the father, grandfather, and greatgrandfather of each candidate. A tabulation of this information indicates that of the successful candidates

in 1148 and in 1256, over half could show no public officials of civil service status among the above-named antecedents.

The testimony of these lists has particular interest because the two years in question fall within a key period of Chinese institutional history. Confucianism was at the peak of its influence—Chu Hsi, in fact, received his *chin-shih* degree in 1148 —and the Confucian theory of government had achieved, under the Sung house, a degree of orderly and stable embodiment it scarcely found at any other time, before or after.

The present article will make a preliminary enquiry into the history and reliability of the two examination lists, present briefly some of the conclusions they suggest concerning the examination system, and propose a reconciliation of their evidence with that of the biographies in the dynastic histories.

2. SOURCE AND TRANSMISSION OF THE EXAMINATION LISTS

The examination lists of 1148 and 1256 are the sole remaining examples of an extensive series produced from the T'ang period through the Sung. . . .

The reason why the lists of 1148 and 1256 were preserved, while those of other years were allowed to disappear, is evident. The list of 1148 contained the name of the philosopher Chu Hsi—humbly placed in the fifth group, number 90. The graduates of 1256 included three men almost as highly revered in China—Wên T'ien-hsiang, Hsieh Fang-tê, and Lu Hsiu-fu. . . .

3. THE CONTENT AND ACCURACY OF THE LISTS OF 1148 AND 1256

Of the two lists, that of 1148 is more precise in its statements, shows fewer lacunae, and proves much the more valuable for our purpose. It lists the graduates (*chin-shih*) of that year according to the five groups or *chia* in which, according to Sung practice, they were rated on the basis of their excellence. The first group was the highest. . . . The numbers of men in each group are as follows:

1st group	10
2nd group	19
3rd group	37
4th group	122
5th group	142

The total number in the five groups is 330 men. . . .

Under the name of each man in the list there is entered, according to a set form, pertinent biographical information, which includes his *tzŭ* [courtesy name] and other names and appellations, his age, day of birth, mother's maiden surname, wife's maiden surname, number of brothers (and sometimes office or degree held by them), legal residence, temporary residence, and certain other facts. Most important for our present purpose, under each man's name there is recorded the name of his father, paternal grandfather, and paternal great-grandfather. Under each of these, there appears a statement of the office (presumably the highest) he had held or was currently holding. If he had not held or was not holding any office, the fact is explicitly stated. In some cases, we are told merely that he has held office (unspecified). In a small proportion of cases only—some 51 out of the 330—does the list fail to state specifically whether or not one or more of the forebears had held office. . . .

For most of the graduates listed, the list itself provides the only surviving biographical data. Only a few, naturally, fell within the small fraction of civil servants whose attainments won them a place in the biographies of the dynastic history or other biographical repertories of the period. In order to test the general accuracy of biographical information in the list, I have made spot-checks in the cases of sixteen men. These were not selected entirely at random. Men at the top of the list and those otherwise known to have attained some prominence were preferred, in the greater hope of finding parallel information

on them. Preference was given also to men who, according to the list, had one or more forebears without civil service records, in order to test the accuracy of such negative statements. In each case selected, biographies of fathers, grandfathers, and great-grandfathers were similarly checked, with particular attention to their service or non-service in the government. Each of ten biographical sources was checked for evidence corroborating or contradicting the statements of the list on the individuals or their forebears.

The result has in general confirmed the accuracy of the list. Independent information was found in nine of the sixteen cases checked. Statements corroborating those of the list were found in all nine cases. In one case only an item seemingly inconsistent with the statements of the list was also found, and this did not bear on family background. . . . A complete check of biographical sources for all 330 names would of course be desirable, but until this is possible, we are justified in accepting the general accuracy of statements in the list.

When we examine the second list—that of 1256—we find that the evidence provided us, though somewhat less satisfactory, is most valuable as a check on the statistics of 1148. The list of 1256 again arrays the graduates in five groups according to their examination showings, and numbers them within each group. . . . According to the list, 601 men received degrees in this year, in the following distribution:

1st group	21
2nd group	40
3rd group	79
4th group	248
5th group	213

. . . For this late period in the Sung, our parallel sources are fragmentary. The Mongol conquest, substantially completed within two decades thereafter, prevented the scholarly compilation and sifting of records until the archives had been largely scattered by war. We have, therefore, no confirmation of the number who received degrees in 1256.

The data of the list on men who passed the examinations are similar to those of 1148, but the later document has clearly suffered more in the course of transmission. Items of information are often omitted; sometimes whole entries, including the name of the man passing the examination, are blank. All entries after number 189 of the fifth group are missing. The list of 1256 does not state specifically when the forebears of a graduate held no office; it

merely omits the official title or the word "served" in such instances. We cannot tell whether some of these omissions may indicate mere lack of information, rather than lack of official service on the part of a given forebear, but I have found no biographical evidence of official service when the list did not mention it.

Parallel evidence on the individuals who passed the examination of 1256 is less abundant than on 1148. Of eleven cases checked (using the same procedure as for the 1148 list), independent biographical evidence was found in four. Support for

TABLE 1. NUMBER OF CIVIL SERVICE EXAMINATION GRADUATES
HAVING FOREBEARS IN THE CIVIL SERVICE

Categories	Examination of 1148						Examination of 1256					
	Group					Total	Group					Total
	1	2	3	4	5		1	2	3	4	5	
A. Total graduates	10	19	37	122	142	330	21	40	79	248	213	601
B. Information incomplete*	0	2	2	15	32	51	0	0	0	0	29	29
C. Total with full information	10	17	35	107	110	279	21	40	79	248	184	572
D. Graduates with no forebears in civil service	4	9	23	54	67	157	8	26	32	131	134	331
E. Graduates with forebears in civil service	6	8	12	53	43	122	13	14	47	117	50	241
1. Father, grandfather and great-grandfather	2	1	5	26	11	45	3	3	11	10	3	30
2. Father and grandfather	0	3	1	6	7	17	0	2	2	13	5	22
3. Father and great-grandfather	0	0	0	2	3	5	0	1	6	12	2	21
4. Grandfather and great-grandfather	2	0	0	1	1	4	2	1	5	15	4	27
5. Father	1	3	3	8	11	26	6	1	7	32	17	63
6. Grandfather	0	1	1	6	6	14	0	1	5	13	7	26
7. Great-grandfather	1	0	2	4	4	11	2	5	11	22	12	52

* This item represents, for 1148, cases in which no definite statement is made on service of one forebear or more, as explained below; for 1256, only cases where entire entry is missing are here included.

the statements of the list was found in all four cases. In one of these cases, that of Hsieh Fang-tê, one minor divergence was found. In another, that of Lu Hsiu-fu, biographers differ on the date of his birth as well as on that of his *chin-shih* examination; but the seemingly sounder source supports the list of 1256.

Such independent information as we have, then, favors the general accuracy of the 1256 list. While less strongly supported by independent evidence than the 1148 list, it remains an unchallenged witness.

4. THE TESTIMONY OF THE EXAMINATION LISTS CONCERNING THE FAMILY BACKGROUNDS OF THE CHIN-SHIH

A tabulation of the information on family antecedents of graduates for the two years yields the figures which are given in detail in table [1].

Simplifying the tabulation somewhat, and reducing the numbers to percentages, we reach the following result:

markable similarity of social composition of the two classes, separated in time by more than a century. Because of the above-noted lack of definite statements where ancestors had not held office, the 1256 list would by itself have limited value as evidence. But its close conformity, insofar as information is given, with the testimony of the 1148 list adds immeasurably to the value of the latter. It both supports the reliability of the 1148 list, and suggests that the situation for 1148 was generally characteristic of the Southern Sung period, and perhaps earlier periods as well.

The similarity of the two years extends beyond general averages to points of detail. Note, for example, the similarity in the percentages of men with official background in the first group. In each year, the men with official background made a much better showing in this group than in the examination as a whole. This may reflect the advantage of superior educational facilities to prosperous officials' sons, when

TABLE 2. PROPORTION OF OFFICIAL BACKGROUND AMONG CIVIL SERVICE
EXAMINATION GRADUATES
(per cent within each group)

Strength of official tradition	Examination of 1148						Examination of 1256					
	Group					Total	Group					Total
	1	2	3	4	5		1	2	3	4	5	
	%	%	%	%	%	%	%	%	%	%	%	%
Prevalent (1+2+3)	20.0	23.5	17.1	31.8	19.1	24.0	14.3	15.0	24.1	14.1	5.4	12.8
Strong (4+5)	30.0	17.6	8.6	8.4	10.9	10.8	38.1	5.0	15.2	19.0	11.4	15.7
Minor (6+7)	10.0	5.9	8.6	9.3	9.1	9.0	9.5	15.0	20.3	14.1	10.3	13.6
None (D)	40.0	52.9	65.7	50.5	60.9	56.3	38.1	65.0	40.5	52.8	72.8	57.9
Total (C)	100.0	100.0	100.0	100.0	100.0	100.0	100.0	100.0	100.0	100.0	100.0	100.0

Two facts emerge strikingly from the above tables. The first is the high proportion of men with no apparent official family tradition whatever. The second is the re-

they were sufficiently gifted and ambitious to profit therefrom. Examples like that of Ou-yang Hsiu suggest that a family tradition of scholarship and exposure in the home to discussion of political problems also played an important role in preparing for later success in government under the Sung: early fatherless, brought up in poverty, taught by his mother, he won in 1030 the first place in the preliminary examination at the capital and not only became one of China's greatest writers, but rose to governmental positions of the highest influence.[1]

In both 1148 and 1256, the men without official background made a much better showing in the following groups—the third in 1148, the second in 1256. The men with very strong official background, on the other hand, tended to make their strongest showing in still lower groups— the fourth group (1148) or the third (1256). Of the forty-five men who in 1148 could show official service for all three forebears, no less than nineteen were in the lower half of the fourth group. Of the thirty men who in 1256 showed three forebear-officials, twenty-one fell in the third and fourth groups. It is interesting also to find in the lower groups men descended from holders of the very highest offices of the Empire. Finally, in the fifth group we find once more a predominance of men with no official background—perhaps including many of slender resources who had achieved their education only with difficulty, and without the aid of well-qualified teachers.

The figures for 1256 would seem to indicate a very slightly higher proportion of graduates without official background than there was in 1148. This may, however, be somewhat deceptive, as it is possible that

our tabulation includes among those of nonofficial background some men with unrecorded official ancestry. In the list of 1148, this danger has been avoided by excluding from consideration cases in which no definite statement was made on the subject. The 1256 estimate of new blood is therefore in this sense a maximum, and that for 1148 a minimum. The actual proportion of non-official family background may have been somewhat less than 58 per cent in 1256, and higher than 56 per cent in 1148.

It may be noted also that we have at hand information only on the paternal ancestry of the graduates. What of the maternal line? There is very little evidence to suggest how similar data on maternal ancestry might affect our figures. But considering the tendency toward intermarriage between the children of governmental officials, it does not seem likely that such data would significantly alter the basic picture. . . .

Unless we find other and more convincing evidence to the contrary, we must accept the conclusion that the examinations of this period regularly served to recruit into the governmental service a very significant proportion of new blood.

5. IMPORTANCE OF THE CHIN-SHIH IN THE CIVIL SERVICE

How much was the composition of the civil service affected by the men of non-official background taken in through the examinations? And how important was the role of these *novi homines* in the government? An answer to these questions in quantitative terms must remain tentative for the present. We know that in addition to the men recruited through the examinations, others were recruited through transfer from the ranks of the military officials, through selection from among the governmental employees holding lower positions not considered to be in the civil service, through degrees occasionally conferred by special grace on those who had taken exam-

[1] Biological inheritance may, of course, also have been a factor in the success of officials' descendants. It does not appear that partiality of examiners accounted for it. Special precautions against favor in grading examination papers were taken after 992, and it seems that they were, on the whole, effective. . . . Apart from individual cases of examination candidates known, like Ouyang Hsiu, for their poverty, or of others known by chance to be well-to-do, there appears at present to be no direct evidence on the economic status of the average Sung candidate or the relation of such status to academic achievement.

inations unsuccessfully a number of times, and through the practice of *yin-pu*.[2] The last was a privilege regularly accorded to certain higher officials, by which they were permitted to designate for entrance into the civil service, without examination, a specified number of relatives, and in certain cases non-relatives. I know of no statistics giving the total numbers taken into the civil service through these several methods. Estimates of the total numbers of officials in certain periods of the Sung have, however, come down to us, and they enable us to form at least a general idea of the role of the examinations in supplying recruits. In the period 1165 to 1173, we are told, the civil officials of the higher class numbered between three and four thousand, while those of the lower ranks of the civil service (not to be confused with non-civil service employees) numbered from seven to eight thousand. If we may hazard a guess that these officials served an average of some thirty years each (the examinations were passed by men commonly ranging in age from the twenties to the

[2] Dr. Wittfogel's article on "Public Office in the Liao and the Chinese Examination System" [reproduced in part below, pp. 34–40] appeared after the completion of the present article. Incidentally to the Liao study, the former article presents some data on *yin-pu* in the T'ang, Sung, and Ming dynasties which supplement the data here presented on that subject. With certain reservations on some of his inferences, I believe that his data in general accord with the conclusions here advanced. Note especially the tabulation on p. 36, which suggests interestingly the relative insufficiency of *yin-pu* for the attainment of important position during the T'ang.

For the Sung, a similar biographic study would be helpful as an independent check on figures otherwise reached concerning the relative importance of various recruitment methods. The information thus far made available certainly does not establish that *yin-pu* candidates in the Sung received preferential consideration for advancement to high office. . . .

As Dr. Wittfogel makes clear, the place of the examinations under the Liao and other non-Chinese rulers differed from that under Chinese dynasties. While of extreme interest for the study of such alien rulers, generalizations concerning the examination system under foreign dynasties may be applied to the Chinese institution only with great caution.

fifties), we find that it would be necessary to recruit some ten to twelve thousand men for the service during the space of thirty years. During the thirty years beginning in 1142, the number of men passing the examinations (apart from degrees by special grace) was 4,428. These could, then, supply some 37 per cent to 44 per cent of the average number of replacements. Thus a considerable accession to the civil service of men without official background was made possible by the examinations, and it should be remembered that an additional number of such men presumably entered the service by other methods.

When we turn from the question of numbers to that of the influence of the examination graduates, we find that it was much greater than these numbers would indicate. Advancement to the more important governmental positions was difficult for those who lacked the scholarly certification afforded by the examinations. Those who had entered the civil service by other means found it still desirable to take the examinations if they were ambitious to play an important role in the government. The list of 1148, for example, includes at least twenty-four men who already held civil service rank, acquired by some one of the other possible methods, when they took the *chin-shih* examination. Five such cases are indicated in the list of 1256, and it is clear that these are not all there were. Even those who entered the civil service through *yin-pu,* although relatives or protégés of important officials, still found the examinations important to their careers, and it was not uncommon for such men later to take their *chin-shih* degree.

We have seen then, that a majority of the men passing the examinations, on the evidence of 1148 and 1256, came from non-official families. We have seen also that the examinations probably supplied at this time somewhere between a third and half of the numbers in the civil service, and filled a still more significant role in supplying men for the more important positions in the government. From these two facts, we might logically assume that a very large share of the higher governmental positions would be in the hands of the *novi homines*. Yet as we noted at the beginning of this article, a survey of biographical information on Chinese officials, including the years with which we are concerned, indicates that the civil service "reproduced itself more or less from its own ranks." How are these two conclusions to be reconciled?

I believe that they are not so contradictory as they seem. The two sets of evidence involve in fact two quite different groups of officials. The examination lists give us a cross section, at two points, of the entire body of men passing the civil service examinations. The biographies, on the other hand, treat only the topmost elite of the Chinese officialdom—men especially noted for their administrative achievements (or outstanding villainies), or officials who won notice through their literary, scholarly, or artistic accomplishments. In the Sung dynasty, with which we are now concerned, the biographies in the dynastic history can scarcely have included one per cent of the men in the civil service during the period.

If this elite contained a higher proportion of men with official background than did the rest of the service, we need not be surprised. Such men had the advantage of political *savoir-faire*. The more prosperous of them had leisure in youth to cultivate the arts. And we have seen that their scholarly records were especially high: in the 1148 and 1256 examination lists, the descendants of officials comprised 60 per cent and 62 per cent respectively of the first group, while they constituted only 44 per cent and 42 per cent of the graduates as a whole. Possible reasons for this have been mentioned. But the sons of non-official families, on the other hand, composed in 1256 65 per cent of the second examination group, and in 1148 66 per cent of the third. It is probable that among officials of importance apart from the small elite represented in the dynastic biographies, they made a much better showing. . . .

Meanwhile it is clear from the evidence already available that in this period graduates who had no family tradition of civil service played, by virtue both of their numbers and of their official functions, a highly significant part.

City and Village: The Inequality of Opportunity

P'AN KUANG-TAN AND FEI HSIAO-T'UNG

P'an Kuang-tan and Fei Hsiao-t'ung are pioneers of modern social science in China. Both have worked in sociology and anthropology. Their basic question and their materials are similar to Professor Kracke's, but their analysis of the data reflects the concern with rural sociology and with the status of the peasant in Chinese society that has colored so much of modern Chinese intellectual and political life.

The article appeared in one of China's leading sociological journals, *Social Science (She-Hui K'e Hsüeh).*

1. PREFACE

The civil service examination system was, historically, the most important device for the selection of officials in China. While the content of the examination might differ from one age to another, basically it was the examination method through which offices were bestowed on worthy men of talent. The selection of officials, to be sure, was not limited to the examination method; that method, however, was considered the normal path to office in the traditional society, because the great majority of the people, except for certain classes of people who engaged in mean occupations and were considered "riffraff," were as a rule entitled to compete in the examinations. The general intent of the examination system to open a career to talent was, of course, incompatible with the principle of determining a person's ability on the basis of heredity. Especially for people of ordinary backgrounds, who sought official employment, the examination system became the direct path to their goal, and to pass the examinations be-

came an end that many strove after. At the same time, through the use of written examinations, the examination system secured a career in state and society for the educated man. The social values fostered by the examination system are well illustrated by such proverbs as: "Overnight, the poor student becomes a somebody," and "All walks of life are lowly, only the scholar stands high." Even today, all aspects of Chinese society still show signs of this tradition.

No matter what the examination system meant to most people, or was believed to accomplish, the degree to which it furthered social mobility is still an open question. On this issue, many differing viewpoints have been expressed.

One side holds that the absence of clear-cut class differences in traditional Chinese society was due to the examination system which continuously selected men of talent from the lower classes and advanced them to a higher position. During the Wei and Chin dynasties [3rd–5th centuries, A.D.], when officials were not selected by general

From P'an Kuang-tan and Fei Hsiao-t'ung, "K'e-chü yü she-hui liu-tung" (The Examination System and Social Mobility), *She-Hui K'e-Hsüeh* (Social Science), IV (1947), 1–21. [For assistance in the translation the editor would like to thank Mr. Liu Ming in Taichung (Taiwan) and Mrs. Dorothy Shou in Poughkeepsie.]

examinations, a society of rigid social divisions and no social mobility developed. In later times, when recruitment was through general examinations, this type of society disappeared.

A contrary viewpoint holds that people who have to work for a living and have no chance to study will naturally have no opportunity to compete in the examinations; even in scholarly families, this argument continues, an individual will find it difficult to pass the examination and obtain a post, unless one's father or brother has rank or reputation and is familiar with the contents and procedure of the examination. Even if such a person passed the first examination, his promotion would be difficult. The best thing for him to do is to return to his village and become a teacher. In this view, then, the examination system does not "bestow rank on worthy students," and it becomes quite clear why official posts are still occupied by a small group of prominent families. The examination system serves only to trap the scholars' ambitions and is not really an effective ladder for social mobility.

Both viewpoints have some basis in fact. On the one hand there are many examples in Chinese history of persons who "after ten years of hard study, entered the dragon gate." On the other hand, since the number of official positions was limited and the examination methods often rigid and the materials narrowly restricted, there existed in fact many limitations on mobility, aside from a person's legal qualification to compete in the examinations, and it was inevitable that the selection of officials was biased. Social mobility existed more in name than in fact. But when we study China's social structure, we cannot follow our own notions and base our theories arbitrarily on partial evidence. We have to make a comparatively accurate estimate of the examination system and its contribution to social mobility. This article proposes to explore that question.

2. THE EVIDENCE

The evidence used in this study consists of 915 so-called "Vermilion-Ink Essays" from the Ch'ing period, beginning with the reign of K'ang-hsi [1661–1722] to that of Hsüan-t'ung [1908–1912]. According to the customs of the times, all the *kung-sheng, chü-jen* and *chin-shih* who had passed the *yu-kung, pa-kung, hsiang-shih* and *hui-shih* examinations tried to print their examination essays and to circulate them among their friends and relatives. Since the texts of the *yu-kung, pa-kung,* and *hsiang-shih* essays were printed in black, they are called "Ink Essays." The *hui-shih* essay, being printed in red, was referred to as "Vermilion Essay." After an initial screening, we arrived at a total of 915 essays. In the time span mentioned above, the total number of graduates of these ranks was of course very large. It cannot be estimated at present. According to a recent compilation, there were graduated during this period 26,747 *chin-shih* alone; the number of the other degree holders was far larger. The material we analyze in this article is thus only a very small part of the total; it is in fact no more than a sample. The materials used were all collected in Peking, and some bias in regard to the periods and regions represented by the essay writers could not be avoided. Still, Peking was the Ch'ing capital and the place where the *hui-shih* examination and the *hsiang-shih* examination for the Shun-t'ien district [i.e. the capital] were held. Moreover, since the purpose of circulating the essays was to make friends and to recommend oneself with an eye to one's career, Peking was the center for the circulation of such essays. The materials we obtained were therefore relatively representative as far as the different regions of the empire are concerned. As for the time span covered, the bulk of the material comes from the T'ung-chih and Tao-kuang reigns. Because this kind of material cannot be preserved easily, the loss for the earlier reigns is considerable.

The distribution of the writers of the 915 essays, by native place, is as follows:

Chihli (including Shun-t'ien District)	187
Kiangsu	113
Chekiang	104
Shantung	102
Anhui	60
Shansi	57
Honan	51
Fukien	47
Hupei	42
Kiangsi	28
Kwangtung	22
Kweichou	20
Hunan	15
Szechuan	14
Shensi	12
Yünnan	11
Kwangsi	11
Kansu	4
Fengtien	2
Taiwan	1
Military	12

The distribution of essays by reign is as follows:

Hsüan-t'ung	12
Kuang-hsü	506
T'ung-chih	182
Tao-kuang	86
Hsien-feng	80
Chia-ch'ing	26
Ch'ien-lung	13
K'ang-hsi	8
Unknown	2

For the most part, the writers of the Vermilion-Ink Essays had been successful in the examinations. Together with the essays, the writers reproduced the names and comments of the examiners, but these do not interest us here. At the beginning of each essay, there is also a paragraph with information on the writer's background. This record is very detailed: the honors, ranks, and qualifications held by members of the writer's family as well as the candidate's own record of publication are included. It is these data which make the Vermilion-Ink Essays such useful evidence for the study of social mobility.

The material on the writer's background is divided into two parts: data on his family and data on his education. The family data list the native place of the writer's family; the educational data give a record of his schooling. In this way, both the biological and social background are stressed, an emphasis which coincides with our modern awareness of heredity and environment. The data on family are, moreover, divided into an upper and lower column. The upper column contains information on the writer's paternal forebears and their principal wives, including relationships by adoption. The lower column includes forebears in the maternal line, male relatives of the mother's family and their wives, and also female relatives in the paternal line up to the writer's grandfather's generation. Under Chinese family law, it makes good sense to record the relatives in the maternal line and it permits us to reconstruct marriage alliances of families and to trace each family's inherited characteristics. The data on education are divided into three parts: information on the writer's immediate teachers; information on friends or scholars who indirectly contributed to his education; and other formative influences. Some papers furthermore divide the data on teachers and educators into an upper and lower column and add the name of the candidate's patron in the lower column. This material, then, is very useful for a study of the essay writer's thought, learning, and political viewpoints.

The final item concerning the writers' background is a record of their families' places of residence.

The data used in this article include only a small portion of the information supplied in the Vermilion-Ink Essays. We have used the data on the writers' places of residence and the upper column of the family background material, including references to official rank within the writers' families back to the fifth generation.

3. A COMPARISON OF CITY AND VILLAGE

Social mobility generally refers to a change in the individual's position in the social structure. But the term is also often used in a narrow sense: mobility from one social stratum to another. Social strata are differentiated, unequal social classes which, according to the value judgments of the community, are divided into high and low, somewhat like a ladder. All people hope to climb this ladder, but in fact they descend as well as ascend. The process of moving, up or down, is called mobility.

The differentiation into social classes is based not only on the criterion of hereditary nobility, but also on type of occupation, income, living standard, and even residential area. In our traditional society, strata were divided into high and low according to the principle: "All walks of life are lowly, only the scholar stands high." Though we may not accept the strata of scholars, peasants, artisans, and merchants as the only four steps on the ladder, the position of scholars was clearly the highest. Indeed, Mencius' distinction between mental and manual labor was the basic criterion of stratification. This distinction coincides with a division based on economic criteria, between "those who are fed" and "those who feed." In popular parlance, furthermore, this distinction also coincided with that between city and village, between urban resident and country dweller.

If we want to observe the phenomenon of social mobility, and to measure the speed of mobility in quantitative terms, a comparatively convenient way is to measure changes in profession, income, and residential area. First, we want to study the influence of the examination system on social mobility with particular attention to residential area. From the data on the essay writers' places of residence we can determine how many of the candidates, at the different degree levels, came from a city, town, or village background. We posit that the city-bred man is relatively higher in social position than the man brought up in the country. From data on village-bred candidates rising upward through the examination system, we can estimate the speed of social mobility.

But before analyzing the data, we have to discuss the assumption stated above. It is not quite correct to deduce social position from the mere fact of residence in a city or village. In the regional structure of our traditional society, the "city" functioned as the political center of an area. For protection and safeguarding, a city wall was built. In and of itself, the resident of a city did not belong to any particular class. Since the political center often provided the most convenient transport facilities, the city also experienced the greatest commercial development. Warehouses and stores were also gathered in cities because of the protection afforded by city walls. Merchants formed an important element among the urban residents. Therefore the words city and municipality can be combined in one term: "urban municipality" (Ch'eng shih). The population of such a city was comparatively large and the variety of occupations in the city was also great. Among others, there were workers who depended solely on their manual labor for a living. Besides, urban residents in general had fields and land in the city to fall back on in times of siege and self defense. Although they were not self-sufficient in food, they could at least supply their daily needs of vegetables. Therefore we can say that there were peasants in the city. The urban population was, in fact, composed of all social classes.

Another factor to be considered is the structure of the Chinese village and whether it was relatively simple or not. If the inhabitants of villages had all been relatively low-class "rustics," we could estimate social mobility from the number of villagers who advanced with the aid of the examination system. But in reality things were not that simple. As the proverb has it, "For generations a family works in field and study." In some places relatively large landlords did not leave their native places for the city but continued to reside in the country. They employed workers on their fields, or rented out the land and lived on the rent. With free time at their disposal, members of this group could study and take the examinations and serve as officials, without ever having moved their residence to the city. In other regions, the landlords who moved into the city were fairly numerous, both because of the difficulty of self-defense in the countryside and because of the opportunity for advancement available in the city. In such regions, few of the people remaining in the countryside were rich landlords. We can also assume that in places where landholding was highly concentrated in a few hands, economic differentiation was relatively sharp and the social structure of the rural population was comparatively simple. In such areas, residential mobility was more or less equivalent to social mobility.

For technical reasons, we have added the category "town" to the other two divisions in our analysis of the 915 writers' places of residence. In some cases, the writer's place of residence was neither city nor village, but a small town, midway in size between the two. Though the number of these cases is not great, we have added the category and thus made the difference between village and city sharper.

City	398	52.50%
Town	48	6.34%
Country	312	41.16%

At first glance, the difference between the figures for city and country seems small, only one-tenth of the total. But if we keep in mind the ratio between the total population in cities to the total population in the country, the relative difference between our two figures becomes greater. By way of an estimate, Ch'iao Ch'i-ming has said that "the rural population amounts to about 90% of the total population." If the graduates of the examination system had been recruited in proportion to the percentage which each social stratum occupied in the population as a whole, those of rural background should have been 90%. We can therefore deduce from the above figures that the opportunity for residents of the countryside to succeed in the examinations was not as great as for urban residents. Yet at the same time, we must explain that the rural population had some opportunity to use the examination system for upward social mobility.

Who among the rural people was able to use the examination system to move upward? From the materials currently available, we cannot answer this question clearly. But we can hope that some meaningful patterns will emerge from a closer look at a few provinces where relatively full data on the ratio of urban and rural residents are available. The results of our analysis of our authors from seven such provinces are as follows:

Province	City	Town	Country	Record Incomplete	Total
Chihli	94	5	45	43	187
Kiangsu	73	8	16	16	113
Chekiang	46	9	42	7	104
Shantung	36	4	51	11	102
Anhui	21	3	29	7	60
Shansi	12	10	27	8	57
Honan	18	1	26	6	51

Among the 915 essays, data on residence were found in only 758 of the papers. The distribution among city, town, and village was as follows: [see above]

Leaving out the category "Record Incomplete," these figures give the following percentage points for the three types of residential areas:

Province	City	Town	Country
Chihli	65.28	3.47	31.25
Kiangsu	75.25	8.25	16.50
Chekiang	47.42	9.28	43.30
Shantung	39.56	4.40	56.04
Anhui	39.62	5.66	54.71
Shansi	24.49	20.41	55.10
Honan	40.00	2.23	57.77

The percentage of graduates with a rural background is lower in Kiangsu and Chihli than the average of all provinces; three-quarters of the men from Kiangsu, in fact, come from cities. This is probably due to the large number of landlords in that province who had left their homes in the countryside. In Shantung, Shansi, and Honan, the owner-farmers were relatively more numerous; in these provinces, the number of graduates with a rural background is also higher. This indicates that rural residents in these provinces had greater opportunity for upward mobility. That is to say, there were in the country more people who could afford to study and attend the examinations. This explanation does not account for the situation in Chihli. The land system of Chihli was similar to that of Shantung and Honan: owner-farmers were relatively numerous. Yet, in our list, the number of graduates with a rural background is fairly low. This is possibly due to the fact that Chihli included the capital where the officials gathered. Their sons and grandsons often moved their residence to Ta Hsing Hsien and attended the examinations for the first degree in Shun-t'ien. This tends to influence the city/country ratio in that province. In Chekiang, the category "rural" is also relatively low. This is because the northern part of Chekiang belongs to the Tai Hu Valley where the same situation prevailed as in southern Kiangsu.

If this explanation is valid, it indirectly shows that the people who could afford to study, attend examinations and rise upward through the examination system belonged mostly to the landlord class. If the landlords in a given province congregate in cities, the percentage of city-bred graduates for that province will be high; on the contrary, if the landlords remain in the country, the percentage of city-bred graduates for that province will be low. This is really a commonsense explanation. If a man has to earn his living through his own toil, his opportunities to study are few. It is naturally very difficult for him to gain a high social position through the examination system. Thus, before people can use the examination system to move up the social ladder, they must first be in an economic position that does not require them to engage in manual labor. It does not necessarily require that they own land. The economic security can come from business, or from the support of one's clan or relatives. But since China's traditional society was actually based on agriculture, the majority of people who could avoid manual labor were those who owned some amount of land.

4. AN ANALYSIS OF THE FAMILY SYSTEM

We shall now consider data provided in the upper column of the record of the writers' family backgrounds to evaluate the family system from which the successful candidates emerged. If a graduate's father or grandfather already held official degree, then the graduate's success in the examination in fact only maintained the social position of the family; his achievement cannot be considered upward mobility. Only those persons of commoner background, that is, with no degrees or offices in their family, can be considered to be socially mobile.

Depending on the degrees they earned, we have divided the degree holders in our sample into three groups: upper, middle, and lower. The upper group includes holders of the kung-shih and chin-shih degrees; the middle group includes kung-sheng and chü-jen; and the lower group contains all the holders of the sheng-yüan degree. Tabulating the degrees held by fathers of our 915 candidates, we arrived at the following figures:

FATHER WITHOUT RANK			FATHER WITH RANK			
			LOW	MEDIUM	HIGH	TOTAL
	306		289	260	60	609
%		33.44				66.56

For the 306 members of our sample whose fathers had no rank but whose grandfathers were examined, the following distribution of ranks among grandfathers was observed:

Among these 129 individuals who in four parental generations have no degree holders, there are three who have lower-ranking degree holders back in the fifth generation. This leaves us with a group

WITHOUT RANK			WITH RANK			
			LOW	MEDIUM	HIGH	TOTAL
	192		74	32	8	114
%		62.74				37.26
% of total		20.98				

Carrying the examination one generation further for those members of our sample whose fathers and grandfathers held no ranks, we found the following distribution of ranks in the great-grandfathers' generation:

of 122 [*sic*] persons in our sample in whose families over the last five generations no degree holders were to be found. Among our total sample of 915, this constitutes a percentage of 13.33. Our specific answer, then, is as follows: Only a little over ten

WITHOUT RANK			WITH RANK			
			LOW	MEDIUM	HIGH	TOTAL
	152		30	9	1	40
%		79.16				20.84
% of total		16.61				

Carrying the investigation yet another step further, for the 152 members of our sample who have no degree holders among their fathers, grandfathers, or great-grandfathers, an examination of degreeholders among their great-great-grandfathers yielded the following distribution:

per cent of the successful graduates came from families without earlier degree holders! This illustrates the width of the road for mobility which the examination system opened for the common people.

Our conclusion, then, amounts to this: the examination system was not completely

WITHOUT RANK			WITH RANK			
			LOW	MEDIUM	HIGH	TOTAL
	129		16	7	0	23
%		84.87				15.13
% of total		14.09				

monopolized by the families already holding degrees, but at the same time, the opportunity for upward social mobility provided by the examination system was not too great.

It is important to note that 13 per cent of our sample come from families who within five generations produced no degree holders, because this proves that it was possible for those without previous degrees in their families to ascend into the respected classes, to get into officialdom, and obtain a better livelihood. No matter how great this opportunity or how little it was, as long as such mobility was in fact possible, numerous people who could afford to study would work hard to seek advancement along this road.

5. FURTHER DISCUSSION OF THE DIFFERENCE BETWEEN CITY AND COUNTRY

We had given attention to the residential background of our group because of our assumption that residents of the country, by and large, had no ancestors with degrees. But in fact this is not so. Among our 122 whose families in five generations produced no degree holders, the following residential backgrounds were to be found:

City	45
Town	9
Country	47
Unknown	21

This is to say, there is no obvious difference here between city and country. This is also true if we look at the residential background of our whole group and correlate these data with the data on degrees held among their fathers:

In this chart, the percentages for city and country are very similar. This also indicates that all those who ascended through the examination system, no matter whether they come from the city or the country, were similar in family background.

This fact does not mean that the opportunity to move up the social ladder was the same for inhabitants of the city and the country. We have mentioned in the third section, in speaking of the population ratio between city and country, that the opportunity for country people to use the examination system for social mobility was far less than that of city people. That conclusion is not contradicted by the present paragraph, because it is still true that the 90 per cent of the population who lived in the country did not have the economic wherewithal to avail themselves of the examination system for social advancement. Those country people who could afford to study and participate in the examinations resembled in family background the city people who did likewise. As we have said before, and to judge once more on the basis of commonsense, they were landlords or people with some other form of economic power. The social mobility provided by the examination system rested on this economic basis. All people below this economic level who wanted to move upward, had first to reach this economic level; then they could avail themselves of the examination system.

6. DISCUSSION AND CONCLUSION

In this review and discussion of our problem, only one point emerges clearly:

FATHER WITHOUT RANK			FATHER WITH RANK								
			LOW		MIDDLE		HIGH		TOTAL	
	No.	%	No.	%	No.	%	No.	%	No.	%
City	128	32.16	130	32.66	117	29.39	23	5.79	270	67.84
Town	17	35.42	10	20.83	18	37.50	3	6.25	31	64.58
Country	113	36.22	102	32.69	87	27.88	10	3.21	199	63.78
Unknown	48	35.59	47	29.93	38	24.20	24	15.28	109	69.41
Total	306	33.44	289		260		60		609	66.56

in the traditional society, the examination system did serve, to a greater or lesser extent, as an avenue for upward social mobility; it did constitute a series of steps by which people could advance socially.

Our data also permit us to conclude that all kinds of people from different professions and with differing residential backgrounds were theoretically able to participate in the examinations; that is, they were not prevented by law from competing, and there was no social prejudice against their taking the examinations. There was no discrimination between families with degree holders and those without; the road was always open for all who possessed the appropriate ambition and ability.

Up to this point, we have only assumed the presence of ambition and ability; we have not discussed these factors. Social mobility is the mobility of people, that is, the mobility of ambitious people; aside from this, there is no significance to the term. There are many factors which account for a person's ambition: inherited intelligence; the opportunity for education; economic security; leisure. In our analysis of our sample, we have taken for granted native intelligence and education; generally speaking, we recognize that the individuals who passed the examinations were superior in their native intelligence and educational opportunities. Modern psychologists who have studied the old examination system believe that the eight-legged essay and the examination method were, in fact, a kind of intelligence test, in addition to being a test of knowledge and memory. If this is true, then our assumption concerning intelligence and educational opportunity is borne out.

With regard to economic status and leisure, we have indulged in some speculation. If we have used supposition and deduction with regard to these two factors without coming to any definite conclusion, it is because the Vermilion-Ink Essays did not supply any data on these two variables. But with regard to the status of peasants and workers in general, we can say that in times of good harvest they could barely make ends meet, in times of disaster, they could not avoid death. Though there was the "open door" of the examination system, they could not enter. In fact, these people were not even interested in trying to take examinations. This is understandable since, according to our deduction, those who wanted to compete in the examinations first had to secure economic status that gave them leisure to study. Such economic status rested not only on one, but on many bases. Land was the most important among them; of those who competed in the examinations, 80–90 per cent were large or small landlords, and not toiling peasants. The data on personal background in the Vermilion-Ink Essays record that some successful graduates came from a peasant background; but in that case, at least these successful candidates did not themselves work on the farm though other members of their family might. Besides land, commerce also could confer the requisite economic status; but a sizeable portion of businessmen in fact were landlords who resided in cities or towns. They did not differ from those members of the "gentry" who engaged in commerce. There were, of course, those who lacked income from landholding and still wanted to study and participate in the examinations; they had to rely on the help of friends, or that of local government or some public agency. At any rate, they were not numerous. Local gazetteers tell us of local political and educational officials who, much concerned with culture, tried to establish something like modern scholarship funds and to use the interest to advance the education of the poor; but we also learn that these funds were not too numerous and that their management was frequently poor, so that actually few people were able to benefit from such stipends.

We have discussed in a rather superficial manner the different ratios of city and country residents among our successful examination graduates; if we analyze the data carefully, a rather sharp contrast between city and country emerges. The personnel recruited from the city residents by examination was recruited from one-tenth of the total population; the personnel recruited from country residents was recruited from nine-tenths of the population. We have also compared family backgrounds of the individuals in our sample and, after eliminating those cases where degrees and ranks were held among the forebears of our candidates, we have found that the examination system served as an effective instrument for social mobility. Strictly speaking, this is true for only a little more than 13 per cent of our sample.

Can this figure of 13 per cent for those who made effective use of the examination system for social mobility be considered large or small? Was the "door" which the examination system opened for social mobility wide or narrow? Judging from the data, we cannot consider this door wide open. But actually, we cannot draw such a conclusion. We need other data and cases for comparison. We should consider, for example, the establishment of the modern school system after the abolition of the examination system, more than forty years ago. What was the proportion of country residents without degree holders in their families who could rise through the modern high school and college to a high position in society, compared with city people and other people of means? Was it larger than the 13 per cent under the old examination system or smaller?

Another comparison that should be made is with the upward social mobility of gifted people in Western society. There already exist some studies on this subject and we can find two or three examples that are statistically relevant.

In his study of *American Men of Science*, Mr. J. M. Cattell presents the following table:

The category "farming" comes of course closest to our category "peasant." The figure for this category shows that 44.1 per cent of the total American population produced 21.2 per cent of her scientists. Although scientists and Chinese degree holders are obviously two different types of people, they are comparable in that both must necessarily possess intelligence. Both belong to the agricultural population and both live in the country; in these two respects, too, they are similar. From our Chinese sample we have seen that of the examination graduates, 41.6 per cent lived in the country, and 6.31 per cent in towns. Since the town dwellers were in part also peasants, we can perhaps take two-thirds of the above 6.31 per cent and add it to our figure for country residents, which becomes then just under 44 per cent. We have also cited Mr. Ch'iao Ch'i-ming's figure according to which roughly 90 per cent of the Chinese population are peasants. We can say that 90 per cent of China's population produced 44 per cent of her examination candidates, and compare this with 44.1 per cent of the U.S. population which produced 21.2 per cent of American scientists. The two ratios are almost identical.

But since the geographical environments and the human skills in question are not the same, these figures have probably little significance, after all. But there is one aspect of this comparison which we cannot ignore. The United States is a free country; social mobility is higher than in other countries and it is easier for talented people to rise to high positions than in other countries. Yet the proportion of the country's agricultural population which became scientists is not much different from the proportion of China's peasant population which became examination graduates. Is this not strange? Actually, it is not strange.

SOCIAL STRATUM	PERCENTAGE OF SCIENTISTS	PERCENTAGE OF STRATUM IN TOTAL U.S. POPULATION
Free Professions	43.1	3.1
Industry & Commerce	35.7	34.1
Farming	21.2	44.1

Perhaps it is simply that America's social mobility seems high but in fact is not high, while China's social mobility at the time of the examination system seems small but in fact is not small. That is, the ladder for social advancement provided by the examination system for people of talent seems narrow, but in fact it is broad.

There is another study of American men of distinction on which we can draw for comparison. In Mr. E. Clarke's *American Men of Letters,* the following table appears:

SOCIAL STRATUM	PERCENTAGE OF SOCIAL STRATUM REPRESENTED AMONG 1000 FAMOUS MEN OF LETTERS
Free Professions	32.8
Business	15.1
Farming	13.9
Industry	4.3
Unknown	33.4
Total	100.0

In this case, the characteristics of our two groups, "men of letters" and Chinese degree holders, are probably closer than in the other comparison, but percentages are more difficult to compare.

We again emphasize, naturally, the category "farming." The proportion of famous writers produced by the American farming population is only 13.9 per cent, compared with the 21.2 per cent of American scientists recruited from a farm background. This figure is much smaller, and considerably smaller than the 44 per cent of Chinese degree holders. It is almost identical with the percentage of Chinese commoner families who, without degree holders in previous generations, produced an examination graduate. That percentage was 13.3, which was our figure for effective social mobility based on the examination system. Our conclusion is similar to the one stated above: The opportunities for America's rural population to ascend to high position in society are not necessarily many; the opportunities for China's rural population to do so were not necessarily few.

In this connection, it is worth while mentioning another factor. The composition of the American and Chinese farming populations is not the same. In China, most people who could use the examination system for upward mobility were landlords who did not work themselves; only to a small extent did they come from the stratum of actually working landowners, and the group did not include any tenant farmers.

In America, those who rise to become scientists or men of letters probably for the most part also come from a wealthy owner-farmer background. By comparison with China, America's population density is low, and the farmer is relatively prosperous; perhaps chances for social mobility are relatively evenly distributed. In China, the opposite was true of the rural population. The opportunity for social mobility was naturally concentrated in the landlord stratum; there were no opportunities left for owner-farmers and tenants.

But as for the number of people who actually moved up, the 13.33 per cent, the situation in the two countries is about the same. If we think of the 44 per cent, the opportunity in China is somewhat greater than in the United States. There are two ways of stating this difference: first, the intellectual level of China's peasant population is higher than in the U.S., possibly due to the attitude expressed in the slogan: "Overnight, the poor student becomes a somebody." Secondly, the examination system in fact does pick people out for upward social mobility, i.e., it develops effective mobility which other societies lack. Both explanations may be valid. The first cannot be verified at present; as to the second, we believe after our investigation that this is a reasonable viewpoint.

A third study of men of talent which we can draw on for comparison comes from post-revolutionary Russia. On the basis of data analyzed by the eugenics specialist Professor Philiptschenko, Professor P. Sorokin has made the following tabulation:

13.33 per cent for China. But by comparison, our figure of 44 per cent is much larger. It is probably more appropriate to take the 44 per cent for comparison because neither it nor the Russian figure of 14.1 or 15 per cent has been qualified as yet by

FATHER'S PROFESSION	PERCENTAGE OF SCIENTISTS AND SCHOLARS	PERCENTAGE OF LITERARY AND ARTISTIC AUTHORS	PERCENTAGE OF MODERN GREAT SCIENTISTS AND SCHOLARS	PERCENTAGE OF GREATEST SCHOLARS AND SCIENTISTS, MEMBERS OF NATL. ACADEMY OF SCIENCE OF LAST 80 YEARS
Free professions	36.0	44.6	46.0	30.2
Officials	18.2	20.0	8.0	15.5
Military	9.4	7.7	14.0	16.2
Clergy	8.8	1.8	10.0	14.8
Business	13.0	6.7	12.0	5.6
Farming	7.9	9.6	6.0	14.1
Skilled, unskilled labor	2.7	9.6	4.0	3.5
Unknown	4.0	—	—	0.1
Total	100.0	100.0	100.0	100.0

The four percentage figures under "farming" are again most relevant for us. In his table, Professor Sorokin added some footnotes to explain the four figures listed under "farming." He explained that the first three items (7.9, 9.6, and 6.0 per cent) include the figure for landlords, and that the fourth figure for "farming" is composed entirely of landlords. In the fourth column, the figure for "labor" (3.5 per cent) includes the common peasants. Since 80–90 per cent of the data used in this survey date from the imperial Russian period, and since the category of "farming" includes absentee landlords as well as other landlords, the value of the Russian data for comparison with our Chinese material seems much greater than the two sets of American figures. We can say that, no matter what their profession, the number of men of talent recruited from the agricultural population was not large. In the fourth category above, it is comparatively big, 14.1 per cent, and if we added to this the common peasants listed under the category "skilled and unskilled labor," it might well reach 15 per cent which is larger than our

data on the educational background of the families involved.

The society of Imperial Russia and Chinese society in the period of the examination system have something in common, especially the economic condition of peasant life and the pressure exerted to the point of serfdom by landords on peasants. Why, then, was the Chinese rural population's opportunity for social mobility so much greater, possibly more than three times greater? We cannot say that it was a difference in intelligence; we just do not know at all. But it seems reasonable to say that it was due to the greater pressure and more severe restrictions imposed on the Russian peasantry by their landlords and due to the presence in China of such a comparatively open road for upward social mobility as the examination system. The validity of this explanation can be confirmed by data on changes in post-revolutionary Russia. With the removal of oppression, mobility would become greater and the proportion of men of talent recruited from the peasantry would become larger. Philiptschenko's kind of analysis may already have been carried forward in time, but we unfortunately do not know of any such studies, if they do exist.

Finally, we quote the conclusions of a Western social scientist concerning the relation between peasant background and human talent. We know from the studies of the two or three researchers quoted above that in some parts of Western society the peasant population does produce some men of talent. The chief conclusion which emerges is, however, that ever since the growth of cities in the West, beginning 400 years ago, it has been only in the city that talent has been recruited. Gifted and ambitious people must move to the city before they can experience upward social mobility. In his work on social mobility, Sorokin has said:

Since the growth of cities, they have almost completely monopolized the function of social promotion of individuals. All channels of social promotion have been concentrated in the city. Unless he migrates to the city, a man of humble origin in the country has almost ceased to have any chance to climb. Even if in a few cases a man, while staying in the country, has succeeded in making money or doing something prominent, such

a man, in order to become really prominent, has to get the sanction of the city authorities. A rich peasant is still only a peasant; a wonderful country poet without the sanction of the city press and the city is still only the poet of "his neighborhood," not known in the world.

This is the general situation in the West. It differs from that of China in the period of the examination system. In China, a country dweller did not need to move to the city or town first. There are many examples of those who succeeded in the examination after years of hard study. To study in the city or town, and to take one's examination there, meant of course to leave one's native place; but this was only for a short time and did not involve moving away from one's native place or original home. Even after succeeding in the examinations for the *hsiu-ts'ai, chü-jen,* and *chin-shih* degrees, a man could still remain a man of the country. A country dweller whose family remained on the land generation after generation still had a great deal of opportunity for upward social mobility. This, it must be said, was due to the examination system.

Merit and Money

CHANG CHUNG-LI

Professor Chang Chung-li who teaches at the University of Washington has specialized in the study of the Chinese gentry, especially in the nineteenth century. Here he presents his views on recruitment into the Chinese elite. The special conditions of the late Ch'ing period and his own interest in the economic implications of gentry power combine to make Professor Chang especially conscious of the role of wealth in the acquisition of gentry status. The selection falls into three parts: the first two examine the role of wealth in the examination system; the third explores the proportion of "newcomers" and members of "established gentry" families among degree holders, with special attention to the use of money for purchase of degrees.

Professor Chang's conclusions underline that recruitment of "new men" into officialdom was by no means identical with recruitment of "men of talent." To determine whether "men of talent" were indeed recruited into the civil service, we have to investigate not only the social backgrounds of graduates, but also the recruitment paths taken by a majority at any given time.

THE SO-CALLED "SPIRIT OF EQUALITY" IN THE EXAMINATION SYSTEM

It has been said that the examination system lasted for more than a thousand years because of its "spirit of equality." In theory, the way was open for any commoner to rise to gentry status and official position. The examination system did indeed make possible a certain "equality of opportunity," but the advantages were heavily in favor of those who had wealth and influence.

One social group was entirely excluded. Members of families of slaves, servants, prostitutes, entertainers, lictors, and others classified among the "mean people" were forbidden to participate in the examinations.

Many exceptions to the principle of equality can also be seen within the examination system. For instance, *chü-jen* degrees or official positions were sometimes granted to sons or grandsons of high officials, to those who detected and reported rebellious activities, or to those who contributed to the military fund or were active in relief work. Some could thus obtain degree or office through imperial favor without having to compete in the examinations.

The rich had a special advantage in entering the gentry. They could purchase the title of *li-chien-sheng* or *li-kung-sheng* [i.e., *chien-sheng* or *kung-sheng* by purchase] and thus skip the *t'ung-shih*, the examination for admitting *sheng-yüan*. They could then directly participate in the provincial examinations leading to the *chü-jen* degree. . . .

The provincial examinations also gave

From Chang Chung-li, *The Chinese Gentry: Studies on Their Role in Nineteenth Century Chinese Society*, University of Washington Press, Seattle, 1955, pp. 182–197, 210, 214–216. Reprinted by permission.

distinct advantage to the sons and brothers of high officials. Their papers were separated from the rest and marked as "official examination papers," and a separate quota was assigned to them. This gave them a very good chance to succeed. This procedure of handling "official examination papers" separately was introduced in 1700. The original purpose was to give poor scholars a better chance, since the results of several earlier examinations had shown that the successful candidates were mostly sons and brothers of high officials. But the practice furthered discrimination instead of correcting it. In setting the quotas, the ministers favored their sons and relatives and assigned them a higher quota. The total quota for each province was fixed. Therefore, the more places that were assigned to the sons of officials, the fewer were the openings available to other candidates. Thus the original intention of helping the poorer scholars became a means for officials' sons and brothers to gain easy admission.

When the papers were first checked, the coexaminers almost always recommended all the "official examination papers" to the chief examiners, while a large proportion of the other papers were eliminated in the first round. Then, as the quota for the "official examination papers" was comparatively high, the participants who qualified under this category had very good chance of success. Many of them could first purchase *kung-sheng* or *chien-sheng* and then easily pass the provincial examination.

With all these advantages leading sons and brothers of high officials to the degree of the *chü-jen,* the high officials could still exert influence and pressure in the metropolitan examinations. After all, the examiners were their colleagues. Such meddling in examinations was especially common in the nineteenth century. It was said that "since Chia-ch'ing and Tao-kuang [1796–1820 and 1821–1850], the heirs of high officials looked upon the examinations as their personal property."

In addition, the bribery and corruption that had always existed in the examinations increased during the nineteenth century. All these factors made for inequality within the examination system.

However, the greatest inequality of all was in the preparation for examinations. The poor simply could not afford to spend many years studying for examinations. There was no public education system. Students preparing for *sheng-yüan* examinations were educated by private tutors or teachers conducting small schools. There were, of course, the *i-hsüeh,* charity schools maintained by the local gentry. However, there is no evidence to show that such schools produced many scholars who participated in and passed the examinations. Most of the poor families needed their sons' help on the farms and could not let them spend long years in study. The preparation for military examinations required expensive equipment, and the poor were therefore especially handicapped in these examinations. . . .

Thus the examination system did not actually afford equal opportunities to all. Wealth, influence, and family background were powerful factors operating for the advantage of special groups. Nevertheless, some opportunity did exist for men without these advantages to rise through their own ability and diligence, and many men did indeed rise in this way. If there was not equality in the examination system, there was a general belief in the "spirit of equality," and this belief together with the fact that some social mobility did exist helped to stabilize the society and maintain the status quo.

However, in the latter half of the nineteenth century, after 1853, the government encouraged people to contribute to the public fund not only by granting the contributors personal rewards, but also by increasing the *sheng-yüan* quota of their native localities and the *chü-jen* quota of their native provinces. Wealthy localities were able to boost their quotas while the quotas of poorer localities remained unchanged.

Finally, as the purchase system was applied on an increasingly wide basis throughout the nineteenth century, many more entered officialdom through the "irregular" [purchase] route. Formerly, the candidates who had passed the higher examinations were promptly assigned to actual offices. Now, not only had the total number of officials increased, but the proportion of "irregulars" had become larger. Many of those who had purchased office were able to obtain appointments to actual posts, while many who had obtained official rank through the "regular" route had to wait a long time for such assignments. As the stream of officials emerging from the purchase system increased, the traditional principle of equality of opportunity through examinations disappeared.

CORRUPTION IN THE EXAMINATION SYSTEM

Regulations were provided to guard against corruption in the examination system. . . .

In actual practice, severe punishments were sometimes imposed during various periods of the dynasty. In 1645, 1652, 1654, and 1657, several officials involved in corruption in metropolitan and provincial examinations were executed and several were deprived of office. . . .

Despite these severe penalties, however, corruption seems to have been ever present in the Ch'ing examination system, although it varied in degree during different periods. . . . In late Ch'ing times, Feng Kuei-fen [scholar-official] stated:

Malpractices in examination are practiced by seven or eight out of ten men. Only one case in several years has been punished according to law. The sages in ruling the world emphasize justice. To have different punishments for the same crime is unjust. What would one say of punishing one out of a thousand guilty of the same crime? Everyone knows it except the Emperor.

Foreign observers also have reported on the matter as follows:

Of late the censors have made a succession of charges against the manner in which the examinations are conducted. One man states that it is not at all unusual for a candidate to throw a copy of the theme, as soon as it is announced, over the wall to a confederate on the other side, who sends back the required essay by the same means. The servants in attendance on the candidates are often professional essay-writers . . . Substitutes are often introduced to impersonate the real candidates. It is true that little consideration is extended to any culprit found guilty of these malpractices; but when the stake to be won is so high, and the chances of discovery are so slight, the temptation is too great to be checked.

Since the names of the candidates did not appear on the examination papers, various subterfuges were employed to identify the papers. In the metropolitan and palace examinations, some candidates often met in a group before the examinations to practice composition and asked the prospective examiners to be critics. The examiners could then recognize their style and calligraphy and would be able to practice favoritism.

The candidates also used other devices to identify their papers when they were sent up for grading. The commonest method was to send the readers slips containing hints on how the papers were written. Needless to say, the readers were rewarded when these candidates succeeded.

A censor reported that in the southeast provinces the copyists who were employed to copy the papers before they were sent up for reading were *chü-jen, kung-sheng,* or *sheng-yüan.* The candidates often bribed these copyists to change sentences or even rewrite the whole papers for them.

Substitutes sometimes came in to take examinations for the examinees, and in one memorial it was reported that even court officials went to take examinations for others. Also, it was not uncommon for a candidate in an examination to write several essays for others in addition to his own paper. In one example, the candidate who did this failed, but the paper he wrote for another won success for that candidate. It has even been said that Li Hung-chang's [statesman of the late 19th century] papers in the metropolitan examination were written by his friend, and both of them succeeded. In a third example, brothers co-operated in the examination hall. Both succeeded in becoming *chü-jen* but were suspected, investigated, and finally deprived of their degrees and punished.

According to regulations, candidates were to be searched before they entered the examination hall, to make sure that they did not bring in books. Later, this regulation existed only in name, and it was said that all candidates brought in books. Discipline was lacking. There was no order when the candidates were entering the examination hall. They were permitted to leave their compartments and were therefore able to communicate with each other. After the examinations were over, revision examinations were held to make sure that successful candidates were really the persons who had participated in the examinations, but these tests do not seem to have been effective. It was reported, for instance, that one person who was still in Shanghai succeeded in the examination held in the capital.

Regulations forbade the "mean people" to participate in examinations. This rule, too, was broken. In the latter part of the nineteenth century, several cases were raised concerning the participation in examinations by sons of gatekeepers and servants of magistrates. Since these were mostly cases of offenders who had succeeded in the examinations, it is likely that the breaking of this regulation was not uncommon.

Despite the fraud and cheating in examinations on the part of the candidates, the situation would have been less serious if the examiners had all been honest. It is true that one of the reasons that members of the Han-lin Academy and the Supervisorate of Imperial Instructions desired to be examiners was that the position was an honored one. Even Li Hung-chang is supposed to have regretted that he had never been an examiner. However, profit was also a very strong motive, as the following quotations show:

The capital, which is supposed to be the model of virtue, is a place which spoils talents. As the country is more and more in a haphazard situation, the worse are the customs and habits. The post of *han-lin* is supposed to be a reservoir of talents but several hundred of them are trying to get assignments as examiners. By becoming such, they will receive supplies from the localities they pass by and presents from various officials.

When a *han-lin* obtains an assignment to supervise examinations, the districts he passes by pay his supplies and the officials send many gifts. When the duty is finished and he goes back to report to the Emperor, when asked about the good and bad practices of the provinces he passes by, he will then not speak the truth.

A friend of mine who holds office in the Han-lin Academy already has white hair and beard. But he still practices examination essays, poetical composition and calligraphy. He sets up timetables to keep himself working as hard as possible. His whole life is as if he were a young student standing beside a strict master. In his words, "If I depart from these practices for one day, I would not be able to obtain assignments to supervise examinations. As *han-lin* but without any assignment as examiner, this is the road to starvation." Later on he actually succeeds in becoming chief examiner for a provincial examination and provincial director-of-studies of one province.

. . . Of course there were upright examiners and provincial directors-of-study. One provincial director-of-studies of the late Tao-kuang [1821–50] period wrote to relatives requesting them not to come to the place where he was holding the examination as he wished to avoid criticism. . . .

A survey of the conduct of provincial directors-of-studies in Kwangtung in the twenty-year period between early T'ung-chih [1862–74] and early Kuang-hsü [1875–1908], as given by a censor who was a native of that province, shows that half of them could be considered as incorrupt while the other half were notorious for corruption, greediness, and inefficiency.

One can conclude, therefore, that corruption was rife in the examination system despite the strong regulations to prevent it and the severe punishments imposed on some offenders. Many examiners and candidates were corrupt although there were also some honest ones. For the examiners, this was their opportunity to profit. For the examinees, the risk of being caught and punished for cheating and bribery was outweighed by the greater chance of success in the examinations. The rewards made the risk worth while. . . .

A QUANTITATIVE ANALYSIS OF BIOGRAPHIES
OF NINETEENTH-CENTURY CHINESE GENTRY

. . . We have attempted to apply a quantitative method of approach to certain material with the intention . . . of exploring some of the questions concerning the social mobility of the gentry as well as the economic basis of the gentry group. . . .

The data used . . . were taken from gentry biographies collected in the voluminous biographical sections of the local histories—the gazetteers of the provinces, prefectures, and districts. Many such compilations were made as late as the nineteenth century, and almost all of them have biographical sections. . . .

. . . Interesting results . . . are seen when we introduce the factor of social mobility into our tabulations. Entrance to the status of gentry was theoretically open to anyone except those belonging to the "mean people." However, it was naturally easier for the sons of gentry to acquire gentry status than it was for the sons of commoners. A study of the mobility of the gentry has then to determine what percentage of the gentry came from gentry families and what percentage came from commoner families. These two groups we have termed respectively "established" gentry and "newcomers." For our purpose it seemed sufficient to establish whether a person's father or grandfather possessed gentry status in order to classify him as "established" gentry. The others are considered "newcomers."

The study of social mobility in nineteenth century China gains a special importance when it is kept in mind that an increasing part of the newcomers came to their gentry status through purchase, the so-called "irregular" way. The regular gentry had to undergo the rigid classical training, though it may be said that with the increase in examination quotas in the middle of the century, the standards of education and discipline were somewhat relaxed.[1] . . .

Some 5,473 cases were studied. Of these it was possible to classify 2,146 as either newcomers or established gentry. Of the cases classified we find that for the whole nineteenth century 35 per cent belong to the group of newcomers. This is quite a high percentage. It might be argued that the compilers of the gazetteers from which these data were taken would have shown a natural predilection toward listing more members of established gentry families than newcomers. We may therefore surmise that the proportion of newcomers was even higher than the cases would indicate.

As far as we can follow the cases in the gazetteers throughout the nineteenth century, the percentage of newcomers increases from 32 per cent during the first half of the century to 37 per cent during the Hsien-feng period [1851–62] and afterwards. Again, the increase shown may be somewhat less than the actual increase because of the subjective element mentioned above.

If we group the cases according to province, we find the highest percentage (65 per cent) of newcomers in Hunan, the home province of Tseng Kuo-fan [impor-

[1] Professor Chang ascribes gentry status to all degree holders from *sheng-yüan* upwards, whether degrees have been earned or purchased. "Regular" gentry status is acquired through examination; "irregular" gentry status through purchase of degrees or offices. [Editor's note]

tant statesman of the mid-nineteenth century]. Obviously this had some relation to the growth of local gentry power connected with the Hunan militia during the middle of the century. Similar conditions may have existed in Kweichow and Yunnan where also within the known cases the percentages of newcomers (55 and 54 per cent respectively) still exceeded that of the established gentry. In the capital province of Chihli, the newcomers also formed a majority (56 per cent). High percentages of newcomers are also shown in the province of Anhwei (47 per cent) and Kwangtung (40 per cent) where the commercial wealth may have accounted for many of the newcomers who mostly entered through purchase.

When we examine the influx of newcomers into the lower and upper strata of the gentry, we note a different development during the various periods.[2] In the Chia-ch'ing period (1796–1820), the proportion of newcomers was 34 per cent among the lower gentry and 32 per cent among the upper gentry, a fairly even distribution of about a third of newcomers in both the upper and the lower group. In the Tao-kuang period (1821–1850), however,

[2] Professor Chang includes in the "upper gentry" all officials (whether by degree or purchase) and all *chin-shih, chü-jen* and "regular" *kung-sheng, i.e.* all officials and all who were qualified for office. In the term "lower gentry," he includes all *sheng-yüan* and *chien-sheng* as well as "irregular" *kung-sheng.* [Editor's note]

a great increase of newcomers is found in the lower gentry (48 per cent), while in the upper gentry the newcomers have dropped to 26 per cent. The total of newcomers in this group as a whole is still about one third, but the percentages indicate the large inroad which the newcomers have made in the lower gentry during this period of deterioration without as yet being able to penetrate into the upper gentry, the core of officials and holders of higher academic degrees. In the Hsien-feng and T'ung-chih periods (1851–61–74) the total percentage of newcomers increases to 37 per cent, but more important still seems to be the shift in distribution of the newcomers among the upper and lower groups. The low percentage in the lower group (24 per cent) and the high one in the upper group (42 per cent) seem to indicate that the newcomers rushed directly into positions of control and influence during the years of civil war. In the last period, Kuang-hsü (1875–1908), the percentage of newcomers in both groups combined remains high (37 per cent), but it becomes somewhat more evenly distributed with 32 per cent in the lower and 38 per cent in the upper gentry group. When at the end of the rebellions the situation had become settled again, a slightly more conservative trend in the proportion can thus be observed, though it may be safely assumed that the total increase of newcomers influenced the quality of the gentry.

Family vs. Merit in the Ming and Ch'ing Dynasties

PING-TI HO

Ping-ti Ho, a specialist in Ming and Ch'ing history, teaches at the University of British Columbia. In this article, Professor Ho returns to the classic approach developed by Professor Kracke in 1947. Working with impressive materials from China's last two dynasties, he examines the social backgrounds of *chin-shih* and *chü-jen* candidates.

IN THE study of social mobility of a historical society such as traditional China's, four methodological problems merit our attention. First, the period should be sufficiently long to allow an observation of the unchanged aspects as well as the changing trends, and the geographical coverage should be sufficiently broad. Any generalization based on local or regional data of a limited and sometimes special period is likely to be risky. Second, statistical data must be cross-sectional. Any generalization derived from dynastic histories and the various biographical series which are inevitably achievement-biased cannot be regarded as conclusive. Biographical sketches in local histories, being often extremely brief, are sources of especially dubious value. Third, the criteria of classification must not be based on neat preconceived theory or theories, for historical facts are so complex that they can seldom be reduced to simple patterns. Fourth, in an age in which there is an insatiable desire to theorize, especially in the Far Eastern field, not all scholars remember that factual control, which requires a laboriously accumulated knowledge of legal, institutional,

economic, and social history, is a prerequisite to any responsible generalization.

With these four methodological problems in mind, this paper tackles an important aspect of social mobility in Ming-Ch'ing China, namely, the entry into bureaucracy. One of the main bodies of sources used is the forty-four available lists of Ming-Ch'ing *chin-shih* collected from the three great Eastern American libraries, the National Central Library at Taipei, Formosa, and the National Library of Peking, which yield a total of 11,239 candidates. In addition, there are 22,785 cases from twenty lists of *chü-jen* (successful candidates of the provincial or intermediate examination) and *kung-sheng* (senior licentiates who much like *chü-jen* had opportunity of minor official appointment). While the *chin-shih* lists cover almost the entire period from 1371 to 1904, the latter lists are confined to the nineteenth century and used as supplementary data. The quality of these lists is generally high as they are not only cross-sectional but provide precise information as to whether the candidate's family had produced any officeholder and/or degree-holder during the

From "The Examination System and Social Mobility in China, 1368–1911," *Proceedings of the 1959 Annual Spring Meeting of the American Ethnological Society*, pp. 60–65. Reprinted by permission of the American Ethnological Society.

28

three preceding generations. Some later Ch'ing lists amount almost to abridged genealogies. These lists are by far the most exact and accurate sources for a study of officials' family background, similar in quality to the two extant Sung lists which form the backbone of Professor Kracke's illuminating article, "Family vs. Merit in Chinese Civil Service Examinations under the Empire."

It ought to be pointed out, however, that our lists theoretically have two defects, namely, the lack of information in many of them on collaterals and the absence of information on the economic status of candidates' families. But thanks to the standardized practice of conferring honorific titles on officials' ancestors, both living and deceased, those candidates whose direct ancestors were not degree-holders or office-holders but whose close collaterals one or two generations before them were holders of office or higher degrees can as a rule be detected. When detected, they are classified as descendants of officials. As to the second theoretical defect, it may have been serious for the period from the founding of the Ming Empire in 1368 [until] 1450, when examinations and recommendations were the two only major channels of sociopolitical mobility. But owing to the serious Tartar invasion of the Peking area in 1450 which resulted in the capture of the reigning emperor, the Ming government began to sell minor official titles, offices, and the title of *chien-sheng,* or Imperial Academy studentships. In the course of time it became increasingly common for men of substantial or even limited means to buy such titles. In late Ming and the entire Ch'ing period it may be said that men of above average economic means almost invariably purchased at least an Imperial Academy studentship which cost between one hundred and two hundred taels of silver. For such a small amount of money they could acquire the right of wearing students' gowns and caps and exemption from corvée, thus differentiating themselves from

ordinary commoners. For a greater part of the five and a half centuries under study, therefore, our data in fact imply some information on the economic status of candidates' families.

In the light of the power structure and the peculiar prestige and value system in Confucian China, we adopt three standards for classifying the 34,032 holders of higher degrees. Group I consists of those candidates whose families had failed to produce any officeholder or degree-holder in the three preceding generations. From our knowledge of legal, institutional, and social history, and also by implication, these candidates may be regarded as coming from families of humble and obscure circumstances. They thus represent cases of very remarkable upward mobility.

Group II consists of candidates whose families during the three preceding generations had produced one or more *sheng-yüan* (holders of the elementary degree) but no officeholder or holder of a higher degree. Since *sheng-yüan* as a class have been regarded by Dr. Chung-li Chang as members of what he calls "gentry," a brief discussion of their legal, social, and economic status is necessary. Legally and institutionally, as is well known, *sheng-yüan* were undergraduates of county and prefectural schools; as such they were subjected to the periodic tests and reviewing examinations supervised by the provincial educational commissioner and had no right to minor government service, a fact so fundamental that it set them apart from higher degree-holders. Being unable to enter government service, *sheng-yüan* as a class, as revealed in social literature and biographies, were forced to make a meager living by "ploughing with the writing brush, tongue, or inkslab" (that is, teaching in village or private schools for a mere pittance), or by taking up sundry trades and lowly jobs, many of which were legally prohibited because they were considered as too derogatory to *sheng-yüan's* status as government students. The frequency with which the modern researcher comes across cases in which *sheng-yüan* gave up their métier for trade reflects that even in their subjective "felicific calculus" there was greater comfort in more adequate living than prolonged material privation often entailed upon them by their students' status. Within the limited space available it is not possible to discuss fully the technicality of *sheng-yüan's* true social status; however, modern students can understand the problem much better if they remember that after the abolition of the civil service examination system in 1905 the time-honored *sheng-yüan* degree was equated by the government with graduation from grade school. While it is true that a *sheng-yüan's* knowledge of basic classics and ability to compose essays were superior to those of twentieth-century grade school graduates, his over-all scholastic standing could not have been higher than that of a modern high school graduate. When the *sheng-yüan* is viewed not in the abstract but against concrete social realities, it is impossible to agree with Dr. Chang that he belonged to the theoretically conceived class of "gentry," albeit an adjective "lower" [is used] to qualify it.

Within certain limits it is permissible to borrow a foreign term to describe a Chinese social class, but when the difference in the social realities behind Ming-Ch'ing *sheng-yüan* and the English gentry is so great, there is reason to reject the term "gentry" entirely in our study of the Chinese society. For in the sixteenth, seventeenth, and eighteenth centuries an English gentry [member] owned anywhere between 1,000 and over 10,000 acres of land, usually dominated local administration, and was as a rule Tory in his political sympathy. Some keen seventeenth-century French observers of English society could find no French or European analogy to members of the English gentry, whom they called "*nobiles minores*," an appellation with aristocratic aroma. That *sheng-yüan* and another comparable group *chien-sheng* (students of

Imperial Academy, only nominal in the overwhelming majority of cases) should be regarded as a socially significant transitional group at all can be justified only because of the premium that the Confucian society attached to bookish learning. Most if not all of the candidates who came from *sheng-yüan* families and constitute our Group II were relatively humble or even poor.

Group III consists of candidates whose families during the three preceding generations had produced one or more officeholders and/or degree-holders higher than and including *kung-sheng*. These families may be regarded as official and potential official families.

Our criteria for Group I are very strict and those for Group III very lenient. If our criteria have a certain bias, the bias should be on the safe side. From the forty-four *chin-shih* lists extant, which comprise 11,239 candidates and cover a period of five and a half centuries, we find that Group I accounts for 29.4 per cent, Group II 12.3 per cent, and Group III 58.3 per cent. The combined percentage of Groups I and II (by our definition nonofficial families) is 41.7 per cent.

For the Ming period alone Group I accounts for 44.9 per cent, Group II a mere 2.6 per cent, and Group III 52.5 per cent. In other words 47.5 per cent of Ming *chin-shih* came from nonofficial families. For the Ch'ing period the percentage of Group I drops to 16.5, which is partially though not adequately compensated for by a sharp increase in Group II, which accounts for 20.1 per cent. The combined percentage of Ch'ing *chin-shih* from nonofficial families is 36.6. The crucial change began with the late sixteenth century, when Group I figures drop from over 50 or the high 40's to below 30 per cent, a trend which continues through the early Ch'ing to 1904. For the nineteenth century the average percentage of Group I is slightly under 16. An analysis of 22,785 nineteenth-century *chü-jen* and *kung-sheng* gives an average of 20.6 per cent for Group I, 27.7

per cent for Group II, and 51.7 per cent for Group III.

Although quantitatively it is not easy to say how much is much, there is reason to believe, in the light of roughly comparable studies of social mobility in Western societies, that the amounts of upward mobility in a greater part of the Ming-Ch'ing period are larger than those of modern Western societies. Even the Ch'ing period, which witnessed a continual decline in our Group I figures because of the more restrictive *chin-shih* quotas and the increasingly keen competition which favored the rich and cultured, the combined percentage of candidates from commoner families was still 36.6, comparable at least to that of lower status Americans who moved into the elite in the twentieth century. Since our Group I represents cases of very remarkable upward mobility and since it accounts for 44.5 per cent of the *chin-shih* of the entire Ming period, the degree and amount of upward social mobility in Ming China are probably hard to surpass by any major society, historical or modern.

The factors which contributed to these substantial amounts of mobility were many and varied. We can barely mention in passing the major ones: the unusually sympathetic attitude on the part of early Ming rulers toward the poor and humble; the establishment of government schools at the county, prefectural, and provincial levels; the rudimentary but nationwide scholarship system; the mushrooming growth of private academies which also offered scholarships to the intelligent and needy; the institution of community chests for the express purpose of subsidizing candidates to travel to provincial and national capitals to take higher level examinations; the availability in many cases of educational and financial aid from kinsmen and friends; the effect of the continual expansion of printing facilities; and the intellectual and social emancipation as a consequence of the teachings of Wang Yang-ming. All in all, Ming-Ch'ing China approached more closely than any previous period to the true ideal of Confucius that "In education there should be no class distinctions."

It would be one-sided, however, to say that the competitive examination system was the only major channel for social mobility. Wealth, as a matter of fact, was becoming increasingly important since 1451, particularly after 1850. This can be shown by our analysis of the initial qualifications of active officials. But viewed from the needs of the whole society and from the necessity of maintaining a balance within the bureaucracy, the sale of offices and titles in later Ming and Ch'ing times, much like the system of *paulette* in France under the *ancien régime*, served a not unuseful social purpose.

In addition to examinations and sale of offices, descendants of high officials could also enter government service through *yin*, that is, hereditary privilege. In sharp contrast to earlier periods, however, the scope of *yin* was greatly curtailed in Ming-Ch'ing times. By Ming-Ch'ing practice only officials of three top ranks were entitled to bring one descendant into state service through *yin* as a seventh, sixth, or fifth ranking official. As shown from biographies the *yin* privilege seldom could go beyond two generations. For the entire nineteenth century those who entered the bureaucracy through *yin* numbered only 942, as against 12,477 *chin-shih* and a much larger number of *chü-jen* and *kung sheng*.

Since the purpose of this paper is to arouse general interest and to invite constructive criticism, I wish to utilize this opportunity to formulate a few tentative generalizations which are based on more than four years' study.

First, for historians the continuity and changes in the social mobility pattern since the permanent institutionalization of the competitive civil service examination system in the late seventh century are worth a brief review. The significance of the examination system [for] social mobility in T'ang times, though quite obvious, as revealed in Professor Ch'en Yin-chüeh's monumental study of T'ang political history, cannot easily be shown statistically because of the lack of sources similar to ours. There seems to have been a remarkable continuity in the social mobility pattern between Sung and Ming times. Professor Kracke's study of the two extant Sung *chin-shih* lists shows that candidates from nonofficial families constituted 56.3 per cent of the total of the class of 1148 and 57.9 per cent of the class of 1256. These figures are highly significant, although they are not strictly comparable to our figures. The main reason is that in Sung times the passing of the provincial examination was merely a requisite for taking the *chin-shih* examination, not a formal degree or qualification for minor official appointment, as it was in Ming-Ch'ing periods. A significant portion of Sung *chin-shih* who are technically classified as from nonofficial families may well fall into our Group III, that is, the broadly and leniently defined official and potential official families. Since the average percentage of Ming *chin-shih* from humble families without officeholders or degree-holders was as high as 44.9 there is reason to believe that the amount of this kind of sociopolitical mobility in Ming times was larger than that during the Sung. This appears all the more reasonable because we know that many channels that promoted upward social mobility, such as government schools, private academies, scholarships, and so forth, were more extensively established after the founding of Ming. In our long-range retrospect, therefore, it may be suggested that the amount of social mobility began to become truly substantial in the Sung, reached its maximum in the greater part of the Ming, started to level off after the late sixteenth century, and continued its downward trend until the final abolition of the examination system in 1905.

Second, in the light of the substantial amounts of social mobility throughout the Ming-Ch'ing period, as compared with those of modern Western societies, it is difficult to say that the civil service examination system failed to serve an important social and political function. Modern students without preconceived theories or prejudice would perhaps rather agree with François Quesnay, a typical eighteenth-century French *philosophe*, who, despite a much idealized picture about China which he acquired from the Jesuits, believed with basically valid reason that by and large the Chinese ruling class was recruited on the basis of individual merit. In fact, the examination system's long history of thirteen centuries is a most eloquent testimonial to its usefulness as a channel of mobility and as a socially and politically stabilizing factor. It is inconceivable for a large nation as pragmatic as China to have perpetuated an institution if it were truly a sham as some modern scholars would have us believe.

Third, as a corollary to the preceding generalization, there is no valid reason to believe that Ming-Ch'ing bureaucracy was a self-perpetuating body. True, the total average of Ming-Ch'ing *chin-shih* from our leniently defined official and potential official families was 58.3 per cent, but the social composition of the bureaucracy was constantly changing. The constantly changing social composition of the bureaucracy was well nigh inevitable because academic success and official appointment owed not so much to blood as to intelligence, assiduity, and perseverance. From our study of the genealogies of some of the most prominent Ming-Ch'ing clans and from extensive social literature, we know that it was very difficult for the average official family to maintain that Confucian puritanical spirit which had accounted so much for its early success. But by far the most important reason for the failure of the bureaucracy to be a self-perpetuating body was the absence of primogeniture and the inevitable process of progressive dilution of family property by the typically Chinese clan and family system. This causal relationship is nowhere more succinctly and piercingly pointed out than by Ke Shou-li, one of the famous censor-generals of the sixteenth century, who, on the occasion of donating some 1,000 *mu* of land as his clan's inalienable common property, remarked: "When the ancient clan system of which primogeniture formed a hard core can no longer be revived, the empire can have no hereditary families; when the empire has no hereditary families, the imperial court can have no hereditary ministers." Small wonder, then, that Ming-Ch'ing China could not have "predestined parliament men" as eighteenth-century England had as a matter of course. Since Ming-Ch'ing China had more institutionalized channels which promoted upward mobility but had practically no institutionalized means to prevent downward mobility, the Ming-Ch'ing society was highly competitive in its own peculiar ways.

Fourth, somewhat different from the gradualness of the processes of social mobility in modern Western societies, our Group I figures and a vast amount of biographical material which cannot be presented here would suggest that there were probably more actual cases of "from rags to riches" in Ming-Ch'ing China than in the modern West, including the United States.

Last, although the amounts of social mobility throughout the Ming-Ch'ing period are substantial by any standard, the significance of the downward trend in our Group I figures must be interpreted in the context of Chinese society at that time. For a nation so used to a "Horatio Alger" sort of social myth, though in a strictly academic and political sense, the steadily shrinking opportunity-structure for the poor and humble must have engendered a great deal of social frustration. It is worth speculating, therefore, whether the persistent downward trend in our Group I figures has had anything to do with social unrest and revolutions that have characterized nineteenth- and twentieth-century China.[1]

[1] This article was in the nature of an interim report on Professor Ho's extensive research on this problem. More complete data and further interpretations are presented in Professor Ho's recent book and in an article which was unfortunately not available for reproduction here. Both these items are listed in the bibliography. [Editor's note]

The Hereditary Privilege vs. Merit

KARL A. WITTFOGEL

Continuing his earlier studies on the *yin* (hereditary) privilege, Karl A. Wittfogel here presents his findings on the recruitment of civil servants under the Liao (907–1125), the great invader dynasty whose state in North China gave the Sung such trouble. Since China has been ruled by invader dynasties for extended periods during the last millennium, the influence of such "dynasties of conquest" on Chinese institutions is of considerable interest for the student of Chinese history.

In the opening pages of his article (omitted here for the sake of brevity), Professor Wittfogel explains that the alien conquerors reserved all key political and military positions for themselves, usually assigning posts to Liao tribesmen on a hereditary basis. In addition, Professor Wittfogel finds, the Liao carried their distrust of examination over into the recruitment of Chinese personnel. After an investigation of Chinese officialdom under the Liao, Professor Wittfogel finds that only a small minority of Chinese office-holders had been recruited through competitive examinations.

I F THIS assumption is correct then the question must be asked: by what other means could a Chinese enter the empire's bureaucratic hierarchy?

Was "purchase of office" (as it has been called incorrectly) or recommendation or simplified examination the easy way to join the bureaucratic hierarchy? Such procedures which time and again occur in Chinese history appeared also under the Liao dynasty: purchase of the right to apply for an office was permitted by law in 1088; and persons of literary attainment might be employed either on the basis of official recommendation or after having passed a simple examination, according to decrees announced in the second half of the eleventh century. But these methods, which were given legal sanction in the latter years of the Liao dynasty, do not explain the great number of Chinese officials who occupied important positions in the tenth as well as in the first half of the eleventh century, apparently without holding a *chin-shih* degree. In some families, few if any members in high positions are credited with having passed the metropolitan (*chin-shih*) or even regional examinations.

Did some kind of hereditary prerogative, comparable to the tribal *shih-hsüan* [hereditary selection] principle, enable a Chinese in the Liao empire to enter upon an official career without fulfilling the examination requirements? Many writers in discussing imperial China have considered the elaborate examination system, which impressed Western visitors in the seventeenth, eighteenth, and nineteenth centuries, a permanent feature of its political organization. For the early period of the empire's history such a theory is patently incorrect; for the later period it needs serious qualification.

From Karl A. Wittfogel, "Public Office in the Liao Dynasty and the Chinese Examination System," *Harvard Journal of Asiatic Studies*, X (1947), pp. 23–33, 35–40. Reprinted by permission.

Under the Han dynasty (207 B.C.–A.D. 220) a candidate for governmental office was examined in regard to character and education. But it was not a candidate's ability to demonstrate his quality that made his candidacy possible. Only when he was recommended by a leading official or sponsored and guaranteed by his father (who himself held an official post) was a young man's eligibility for government service assured. This method was called *jen-tzu*, "to sponsor a son." During the four centuries of political disruption that followed the Han period, the nine ranks of officialdom were set up and elaborated. Positions in these ranks were to a large extent occupied by members of the upper groups, the "hereditary families." The *jen-tzu* system was modified and restricted, but not abandoned. During this era of disunion and open conflict, the states preferred a stable bureaucracy to a more liberally recruited officialdom which might be more efficient but perhaps less reliable.

The reunified China of the Sui and T'ang dynasties presented new administrative problems which could not be satisfactorily solved by a hereditary officialdom. Additional intellectual resources were opened up by the creation of an elaborate examination system, which, in spite of many interruptions and changes, continued to flourish until the end of the Manchu dynasty.

Those who installed the new examination system did not find it incompatible with the old concept of a self-perpetuating bureaucracy; in fact, they pointedly adopted a number of measures that limited the effectiveness of the new and more flexible method of official selection. T'ang regulations dealing with application for office threatened punishment to "the sons of families with criminal records, artisans and merchants, [who belong to] groups other than [the literati and peasants]," and to those with false documents, if they sought government posts.

In classifying the artisans and merchants as undesirable outsiders the T'ang government followed its Sui predecessor, which specifically prohibited these groups from holding office. Whether the T'ang laws actually closed the examinations to artisans and merchants is not clear. The Sung government seems to have permitted them to participate, but it did so with reservations: the "artisans, merchants [being] outside groups," and former Buddhist and Taoist monks were warned not to falsify their family or personal status in their examination documents. Marked as social outsiders, the artisans and merchants were obviously suspect, and, in all probability, were discriminated against.

The restriction governing outsiders was only one way of interfering with the democratic functioning of the examination system. Protective measures were also taken to strengthen and maintain the power of the bureaucratic in-group. The Sui and T'ang dynasties, which established and elaborated the world's greatest system of competitive examinations, were careful to insure access to office to the direct descendants of the acting bureaucracy without examination. This solicitude, and the privilege that resulted from it, technically resembled the Han institution of "sponsoring sons," *jen-tzu*. But in its new social context—the examination system—the old institution assumed a new significance, and not surprisingly, a new name *yin*. *Yin* means "shade, shelter; to protect." The son of an official who entered the civil service through the *yin* privilege was indeed, thanks to his father's position, "protected" against the hardships and pitfalls of the regular examinations. The earlier phrase *jen-tzu* did not completely disappear, but the new term *yin* which had been used on occasion under the Northern Chou dynasty —the last pre-Sui dynasty—acquired increasing importance when the prerogative was systematically elaborated under the Sui and particularly under the T'ang dynasties.

According to regulations in force before 650 and confirmed in 717, the sons of officials in the first three ranks might apply for positions in the seventh rank; those whose fathers held offices in the fourth or fifth ranks could apply for positions in the eighth rank. But the holder of a *chin-shih* degree could only ask for a position in the ninth rank, second class, upper grade, if he had attained top honors; or if he had achieved minor distinction, for a post in the ninth rank, second class, lower grade. Thus the son of a high official, without submitting to any difficult examination, had a definite advantage at the start of his official career over the well-equipped but not "protected" holder of a *chin-shih* degree.

The establishment of the exact percentage of T'ang officials who are known to have entered upon their bureaucratic careers on the basis of the *yin* prerogative must be left to a comprehensive analysis of T'ang society. However, two preliminary samplings have been made from biographical data contained in the *New History of the T'ang Dynasty*. First, the names of 111 leading officials (mostly prime ministers) who held office at different periods during the dynasty were chosen from the chronological tables of the *Chung-kuo Ta-shih Nien-pao*; then their life histories as recorded in the *T'ang Shu* were investigated. The second sampling was obtained from an examination of 153 biographies of officials of different rank who lived during the dynasty's middle period when T'ang institutions were in full flower. The two surveys yielded the following results:

of degrees recorded: 18 to 42. The picture among the leading functionaries is somewhat different. Here the ratio of *yin* officials to those who held the degree is 7 to 86. While, of course, no definite statement is possible at this point, it may be hazarded that appointment to the empire's leading offices was determined in the main by considerations of personal qualification. Officials hardened in competition and of tested ability seem to have had a better chance of achieving the highest positions than the privileged sons who more often obtained posts in the middle or upper middle brackets.

An instructive illustration of the functioning of the *yin* privilege is found in the biographical sketches in *T'ang Shu*. These cover several generations of officials of the Tu family, and show how the high position of one member, Tu Hsi-wang, opened the door to office for his son, Yu. Yu's position benefited his son, Shih-fang, who also possessed the *yin* privilege. Having attained high office, the latter again paved the way for his *yin* son, Ts'ung, who climaxed the family's service record by achieving the post of prime minister. Two other sons of Shih-fang also rose to office: for one, Tao, the method of entry is not specified; Mu held the *chin-shih* degree.

While revealing the obvious advantages of the *yin* privilege for achieving a distinguished governmental career, the biogra-

CATEGORIES	OFFICIALS OF TOP RANK (ALL PERIODS OF THE T'ANG DYNASTY)		OFFICIALS OF ALL RANKS (MIDDLE PERIOD OF THE T'ANG DYNASTY)	
	Number	Percentage of Cases Investigated	Number	Percentage of Cases Investigated
Examination recorded	86	77.5%	42	27.4%
No record of either examination or *yin*	18	16.2%	93	60.8%
Yin privilege	7	6.3%	18	11.8%
Grand Total	111	100%	153	100%

The number of officials in the second category who benefited from the *yin* privilege is impressive; it is even more impressive when seen in relation to the number

phies of the Tu family also indicate its limitations. The prerogative did not carry the holder automatically to the bureaucratic level of his father; furthermore, the number of those who enjoyed the *yin* status seems to have been definitely restricted. These facts explain why many sons and grandsons of officials entered upon a bureaucratic career by way of the *chin-shih* or some similar examination. It also explains why the non-privileged sons of high officials were prone to consider the examination an unmitigated nuisance. The T'ang statesman, Li Te-yü, voiced the discontent of this group when in 840 he said: "The outstanding officials of the court ought to be the sons of the highest officials. Why? Because from childhood on they are accustomed to this kind of position; their eyes are familiar with court affairs; even if they have not been trained in the ceremonial of the palace, they automatically achieve perfection. Scholars of poor families, even if they have an extraordinary talent, are certainly unable to accustom themselves to [its routine]." Obviously pleased with his own *yin* status, which had enabled him to become prime minister twice without the usual examination worries, Li Te-yü proudly pointed to other leading officials who also had never exposed themselves to the exacting tests. . . .

In T'ang times the emphasis placed on hereditary privilege was strong indeed, but under the Sung dynasty the trend assumed still greater vigor. During this fateful period of Chinese history the *yin* privilege was bestowed at the great triennal *chiao* sacrifice, on the emperor's birthday, after the death of a distinguished official, and on a number of other occasions.

During the great earlier dynasty the possession of the *yin* privilege was automatic with certain official positions. The beneficiaries, whose number was restricted to one or two persons, were usually the official's son or grandson. In the Sung period, the potential beneficiaries included all male kin within the *wu fu,* "the five degrees of mourning," as well as relatives bearing a different surname, and even such persons as attendants and physicians who might boast neither blood nor affinal tie. . . . After 1182, when energetic efforts were made to restrict the system, a prime minister might still receive the *yin* privilege for ten individuals.

This policy of repeated honorings greatly increased the total number of *yin* beneficiaries. During the reign of Kao-tsung, that is, in the years following the collapse of the northern part of the Sung empire in 1127, as many as four thousand *yin* prerogatives are said to have been distributed on the occasion of a single *chiao* sacrifice. The figure becomes particularly impressive when it is viewed against the number of successful *chin-shih* candidates in the same critical decade. These successful candidates only averaged between three hundred and four hundred persons, with a maximum of 538 in 1128. Even before 1127, the *chin-shih* total rarely rose above six hundred, the all-time high for Northern Sung being 805 in 1124.

At the end of the twelfth century, successful *chin-shih* candidates averaged in the neighborhood of four hundred persons triennially. To be sure, *yin* claims at this time were conspicuously reduced by the reforms of 1182; yet at the *chiao* sacrifices some three to four hundred individuals still received the *yin* privilege. On the basis of the material just cited and with due allowance for possible exaggeration, it seems fair to say that at best in Sung times the number of persons who might claim office by virtue of the *yin* principle approximated the number of those who succeeded in passing the *chin-shih* examinations. Under emergency conditions the first group seems to have strikingly outnumbered the second. . . .

. . . From the standpoint of the history of the Liao dynasty it is highly significant that the *yin* privilege which influenced the structure of T'ang officialdom to no inconsiderable degree continued to flourish, and to flourish more fully, under the aegis of Sung power. After the fall of the T'ang dynasty, the Liao government adopted a number of Chinese administrative institutions, but only later when the Sung empire was established did these institutions

reach their fullest development. Small wonder, then, that when the Liao rulers set up
their examination system, they restricted its
effectiveness, as had the T'ang and Sung
rulers, by social discrimination on the one
hand and the *yin* prerogative on the other.

No Chinese official of the Liao dynasty
is known to have risen from the ranks of
doctors, diviners, butchers, peddlers, slaves,
unfilial children, or criminal fugitives, all
of whom were excluded from participating
in the examinations by the edict of 1050.
The divergence from the T'ang formula is
clear. Artisans are not mentioned in the
Liao list and the tradesmen who were discriminated against were called *fan*, "peddlers," not *ku* or *shang* as in the analogous
Sui, T'ang, and Sung laws. Was the Liao
measure actually confined to peddlers, or
was the term *fan* used contemptuously to
designate the whole mercantile class? The
order of 1105 was less ambiguous; it marked
as undesirable the families of the more or
less substantial merchants (*shang ku*).
Thus, in certain details the Liao government modified the earlier formula, but in
principle it accepted the T'ang policy of
excluding social outsiders from the *chin-
shih* examinations. By implication it also
excluded them from the offices to which
the examinations led.

The existence of the *yin* privilege can be
clearly demonstrated from the pages of the
Liao Shih, but this history provides little
concrete information on its form and operation. Additional data are available in the
Ch'i-tan Kuo Chih, whose Sung author, at
the close of his description of the Liao examination system, writes: "As to the regulations concerning the sponsoring of sons,
both civil and military officials had to present a request to the throne for the *yin*
prerogative, and the number [of those who
might receive the privilege] was fixed."

This privilege, implicit in the biographies of many outstanding Liao Chinese
officials, persisted until the end of the
dynasty. . . .

Did the *yin* privilege assume unusual
importance in the Chinese administration

of the Liao government? Was its role as
great under Liao rule as under the contemporary Sung dynasty? The Chin [in-
vader dynasty which overthrew the Liao
and further encroached on Sung territory]
critics thought so, and an examination of
the available records tends to confirm their
impression. Obviously, the Ch'i-tan [tribal
name of the Liao] masters were even less
inclined than were their southern rivals to
award high-ranking positions to successful
chin-shih candidates. The reasons for this
policy can easily be imagined. The Liao
empire was dominated by a tribal nobility
which traditionally considered political positions in terms of hereditary prerogatives
—highly flexible, it is true, but prerogatives
nevertheless. The presence of a Chinese
system of official privilege probably attracted more than it repelled the Liao rulers. While personal ability was always a
consideration, it could be determined by
more pragmatic methods than an examination system. The scholarly bureaucracy's
desire to maintain the cherished *chin-shih*
tradition came into conflict with the Ch'i-
tan predisposition not to take the examination system too seriously—although its
value for Chinese administration was not
denied. . . .

The differences between the *shih-hsüan*
[hereditary selection as practiced by the
Ch'i-tan] and the *yin* privileges are obvious. The former, an institution of a relatively simple tribal state, gave members of
a specific family a claim over generations
to a specific office or class of office. The
latter, the product of a complex bureaucratic government, granted a limited number of direct descendants (not a family)
access without examination to an official
career (not to a specific office). The *shih-
hsüan* system, although not applied directly to the Liao Chinese officialdom, may
well have promoted the growth of corresponding trends in the existing Chinese
government institutions. . . .

In the subsequent dynasties of conquest,
members of the ruling nationality were
fitted into a unified political machine, al-

though as a group they continued to maintain their control over it. Under these conditions master nationals were often appointed to office without recourse to examination. Others, with a bow to the system, enjoyed hereditary exemption; while those who exposed themselves to competition found their tests considerably simplified. The tribal holders of hereditary privilege usually enjoyed advantages denied their Chinese rivals, but, interestingly, their prerogative in imitation of the old Chinese institution was called *yin*. In this form the *yin* privilege manifests itself in all post-Liao conquest societies of China—in Chin, in Yüan, and Ch'ing. In each of them, however, it is only one aspect, although a significant aspect, of the larger *yin* institution as it operated in all post-Liao and post-Sung dynasties.

In the northern and southern sections of their newly established empire, the Jurchen [established the Chin dynasty in North and North Central China, 1126–1234] found a pattern of selection which permitted hereditary claims to play almost as important a role as competitive examinations. According to a Chin scholar, Yüan Hao-wen, four out of ten officials came from the ranks of the "sponsored sons." Such an extension of the *yin* system bothered the Chin rulers considerably—however, not so much because it curtailed the chances of successful *chin-shih* candidates, but because it increased the number of potential Chinese officeholders. It is well to remember that the semi-Sinicized Jurchen, who found it unnecessary to set up a separate "northern" government, filled many leading positions within their unified political organization with their own nationals. Yet despite this very natural bias they readily bestowed official favors upon trusted Chinese dignitaries. After the year 1202 an official of the first rank still had the right to place six persons in office because of his *yin* privileges; and the fortunate beneficiaries might still be drawn either from the direct or the collateral line.

The Mongols, like the Ch'i-tan, followed a pastoral way of life; but they exhibited much less understanding of Chinese civilization than had their nomadic predecessors. Their distrust of a politically independent Chinese leadership was consistently expressed by their recourse to methods other than the examination system when selecting Chinese for office. In 1237, shortly after the collapse of Chin power, Yeh-lü Ch'u-ts'ai [1190–1244, chief minister of the rising Mongol state in North China, descendant of the Ch'i-tan royal house] urged the introduction of competitive examinations. The first attempt at realization produced more than four thousand successful candidates, but the plan was soon abandoned as "not convenient." From then on until the time of Kublai Khan, Chinese officials in the service of the Mongol government achieved their positions primarily on the basis of appointment. In 1267, however, when the great Khan came to regard himself as the overlord of the entire Chinese world, the value of establishing an examination system was again discussed, again without any lasting practical results. Instead the government carefully formulated the *yin* principle which, in the forty-six years that followed, constituted the sole rival to position by appointment. During the middle period of Yüan rule a blue print for a new examination system was worked out, but it was accepted only in 1313. Two years later, the much-debated plan was put into operation and, except for a short interlude between 1335 and 1340, it continued to function until the close of the dynasty. The restored examinations, far from putting an end to the *yin* claim, emphasized its importance in a new way: a *yin* beneficiary, who passed the *chin-shih* examination, might enter the official hierarchy one rank higher than his less favored colleagues.

The Liao rulers had been none too eager to adopt the Chinese examination system. The Mongol masters were considerably less so. Even when they took the "democratic" step, the number of successful *chin-shih* candidates remained extremely small: 180

constituted the all-time high, but averages totalled not more than seventy (including a number of "barbarians"), and this within a territory easily larger than the Sung domain and many times larger than the Chinese regions of the Liao empire.

The *chin-shih* figures clearly reveal the Mongol tendency to limit the number of high Chinese officials. The same tendency is disclosed by the regulations dealing with the hereditary claim to office, a claim that otherwise was held in great esteem. During the Yüan period the *yin* privilege could only be bestowed on one son or grandson, or, if there was no direct descendant, on one male collateral. But, as if to compensate for the numerical restriction, the Mongols raised the level of entry into the official hierarchy for *yin* claimants from the seventh to the fifth rank, a level higher than during the T'ang dynasty.

At the outset, the Ming dynasty accepted their predecessor's policy of official selection; but, in the changed political climate, the *yin* principle assumed a markedly different functional significance. Under the Mongols, the limiting of the number of *yin* claims to one was part of a general effort to restrict the number of Chinese in official positions. Under the Ming government the same device greatly enhanced the opportunities of the successful *chin-shih* candidates who, freed from Yüan oppression and suspicion, again totalled several hundred persons triennially. Furthermore, in the year 1467 the Ming rulers limited the claim to the *yin* prerogative to officials within the three highest ranks, a policy that contrasted sharply with the Mongol precedent of granting the hereditary privilege to members of all ranks above the two lowest. But, most important, those who possessed the *yin* prerogative could no longer reach the apex of the hierarchical pyramid, as indeed they had been able to do until the close of the Yüan dynasty. In Ming times the *yin* prerogative assured the holder access only to a minor position in the central government or to the post of prefect in the provincial administration. Occasional appointments to high office excepted, persons eager to attain top-ranking positions had to pass through the gates of the regular examination system.

The Manchus, willing to utilize as many Chinese institutions as political expediency permitted, adopted the *yin* policy of the Ming dynasty with minor restrictions. The *yin* beneficiaries might still fill the office of assistant prefect or magistrate, but they could not become prefects; in the main they were confined to minor positions in the central government.

Our comparative survey of the two Liao types of inherited privilege, the tribal *shih-hsüan* and the Chinese *yin* prerogative, draws attention to three important points:

(1) The Ch'i-tan *shih-hsüan* system ingeniously combined inherited privilege and individual ability. A comparative study of other Inner Asiatic peoples may reveal, either for some or for all of them, a similarly flexible policy governing their "hereditary" officialdom.

(2) The *yin* prerogative was a corollary to the developing examination system. Study of either must include the other; it must also include a consideration of policies that discriminated against undesirable social outsiders.

(3) A special problem arises in dynasties of conquest. As long as the tribal conquerors maintained a dual political order, their hereditary claims to office tended to assert themselves in a form more or less similar to the traditional tribal pattern. However, when the political organization was unified, the prerogatives were adjusted in large degree to the existing Chinese institutions (examinations and *yin*). Thus, the *yin* privilege must be seen as a specific aspect of the Chinese examination system not only in such essentially Chinese dynasties as T'ang, Sung, and Ming, but also in the great periods of conquest, Liao, Chin, Yüan, and Ch'ing.

Patterns of Downward Mobility

FRANCIS L. K. HSÜ

Francis L. K. Hsü, a noted Chinese anthropologist and sociologist, has taught and published in this country for many years. He is at Northwestern University. One of his main interests has been the study of the Chinese family. This interest is reflected in the present article, where Professor Hsü is measuring the ability of families to retain prominence over several generations, on the assumption that a high degree of downward mobility is one measure of a society's upward mobility.

1. THE PROBLEM

Not much is scientifically known about social mobility in China. Most people who discuss the subject, including some serious students, have been impressed by the great imperial examination system which has functioned in China for over a thousand years, which was a model for the development of the civil service examination systems in the West, and which served to build a great empire the administrators of which were chosen by ability and talent.

A number of scholars adhere to a more or less opposite view. This group, though comparatively small, is gaining in importance. The outstanding student among this camp is K. A. Wittfogel, who has up to date presented the only body of quantitative data on the subject. The major observation of this student is that the imperial examination system, far from encouraging vertical mobility, was very much undercut by the *Yin* privilege, through which the son of an official could enter the bureaucracy without having anything to do with the examination system.

The purpose of this paper is to show that the *Yin* privilege notwithstanding, there is substantial evidence in support of the former view, namely that a fairly high degree of social mobility existed in Chinese society during the last thousand years. This will be done by showing that (1) in the majority of cases prominence (chiefly bureaucratic, but also social, economic or literary, as will be made clear below) did not last over one generation; and (2) that of the families which did maintain themselves a little longer, the vast majority did not last over two generations. These facts have led me to the tentative conclusion that there was a considerable degree of vertical social mobility in China, since with no evidence for any drastic reduction of the opportunities of prominence, the families which fell would in the normal course of events be replaced by others which rose.

2. ANALYSIS OF MATERIAL FROM DISTRICT HISTORIES

The material to be presented here represents a partial report of a wider study which is still in progress. The basic data are taken from the biographies contained in Chinese district histories. District histories (sometimes called District Gazetteers) are a well-

From Francis L. K. Hsü, "Social Mobility in China," *American Sociological Review*, XIV (1949), pp. 764–771. Reprinted by permission of the American Sociological Association.

known documentary source to students on China. The vast majority of the nearly two thousand districts in China have such histories. Some of these documents consist of five to ten volumes; others run into thirty, or fifty, or more. Each set of district histories, amongst other things, contains a large or small number of biographies of male natives of the district who have, for one reason or another, achieved some prominence. These histories have been in existence for various lengths of time. Some, like those for Changsha, were first composed in 1871; others, like those for Nan Pi of Hopei province, were made only less than twenty years ago. The ones which began many centuries ago have as a rule been rewritten or recomposed several times by effort of natives of the districts who had reached some social and political height. Many additions of material, including many new biographies, have usually been made with each fresh effort at rewriting or recomposing the district history.

In connection with the local biographies I am first of all concerned with two things: (1) Some men rated individual biographies, others did not; and (2) some men, though not biographees,[1] were mentioned in the biographies of their fathers, brothers, uncles, patrilineal cousins, or other family members, while others were not. For purpose of this study those men who were mentioned in other people's biographies are regarded as having achieved some degree of *prominence* over those whose names were not mentioned in any biography; and those men who rated individual biographies themselves are regarded as having achieved a higher degree of *prominence* over those who were merely mentioned in some biographies. Since the composers of most district histories appear to spare little effort in identifying the ancestry or progeny of all their biographees, particularly the more prominent ones, the assumption is not absurd that those immediate ancestors and

descendants of biographees who were in any way notable would rate separate biographies or be mentioned in their kinsmen's biographies; and that, conversely, those immediate ancestors or descendants who did not rate as individual biographees, nor were mentioned in their kinsmen's biographies, were probably not prominent at all.

Data from four major district histories will be presented here. These are: Chang Sha (Hunan); T'ai An (Shantung); Wu Hsien (Kiangsu); and Sian (Shensi). These four are chosen for presentation here because they represent four widely separated areas and also because of their relative importance in different periods of Chinese history. The data are analyzed in the following ways:

1. First the data are arranged to reveal the proportion of those in each of which only the prominent man himself is mentioned as compared to those biographies which are related to one another by lineal relationship or in each of which other lineal ancestors (such as father) or descendants (such as son) are also mentioned by name. For example, the biography of H. C. Ou of Changsha made no mention of anyone except himself and his achievements; on the other hand the biography of C. Y. Fan of Wu Hsien, Kiangsu, contained some references to his sons, his grandsons and his great-grandsons by name and by achievements. Furthermore, each of Fan's four sons and one of his grandsons rated a separate biography in the same district history. (See Diagram I)

2. Secondly, those biographies which contain references to the biographee's lineal ancestors or descendants by name and by achievements, or which are tied up to each other by lineal relationship, are then analyzed to reveal the number of generations through which prominence lasted. For example, in the biography of M. S. Teng of Wu Hsien, Kiangsu, only his son Hsiu, is mentioned. This is then entered into the results as *one instance* in which family prominence lasted two generations. The same would be true if the son is a separate

---

[1] The term "biographee" signifies in this paper the person whom the biographer writes about in any given biography.

DIAGRAM I

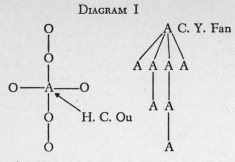

A—a biographee or his kinsmen who has been mentioned in his biography, or who rated separate biographies.

O—a person whose existence is assumed but who is not a biographee nor mentioned in any biography.

biographee. If the sons of Mr. Teng's son were mentioned, or if Mr. Teng's father were mentioned in the same biography or in a different biography, the case will then be entered into the results as *one instance* in which family prominence lasted three generations. (See Diagram II)

DIAGRAM II

A   M. S. Teng   A   Teng's father
| |
A   Hsiu   A   Teng
                         |
                         A   Teng's son

However, three other circumstances are of importance here. For example, Mr. C. C. Pan of Wu Hsien, Kiangsu, not only has a son who is a separate biographee but also two brothers, C. D. and C. T., who are also separate biographees. Furthermore C. T. has one son who is named in C. T.'s biography, while C. D. has a son and a grandson who are also separate biographees. In this case we have three separate lines of continued prominence and accordingly the data are entered in the results as two instances in which family prominence continued for two generations and one in which it continued for three generations. (See Diagram III a)

A different condition prevails in the aforementioned case of C. Y. Fan of Wu Hsien, Kiangsu. The biographies mentioned that Fan had one "seventh genera-

DIAGRAM III a

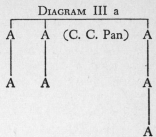

tion grandson," named Pang Cheh who had a son Wen Ying. In addition the biographies also mentioned two other groups of Fan's descendants: 1. a "seventeenth generation descendant," Yun Lin and his son P. Ying: and 2. a "twenty-third generation" descendant Lai Chung and his son Hwa. All three cases are entered into the results as three instances in which family prominence was continued for two generations.

The third condition concerns a rule of thumb. If a father is a biographee or mentioned in a biography, the son is not but the grandson again is, then the case is entered as an instance of continued prominence lasting *two generations*. But if the prominence is interrupted by more than one generation the prominence is considered discontinued. (See Diagram III b)

DIAGRAM III b

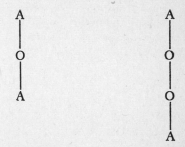

Prominence lasting   Prominence is
two generations   discontinued

3. When the prominence is interrupted by more than one generation the classification of the prominent descendants who

came later on will depend upon whether the sons and grandsons of the later continued the prominence or not. If the descendants mentioned after an interruption of more than one generation had no prominent sons or grandsons they are merely noted in a separate category. In this category are also included prominent brothers, nephews or patrilineal cousins, whose children are not biographees or mentioned in the biographies. (See Diagram IV)

DIAGRAM IV

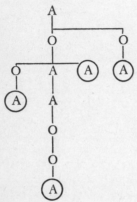

The individuals in circles are grouped together and are then added to the total number of individuals among whom prominence continued for two or more generations.

4. Fourthly the data are arranged to reveal the number of individuals who are related to each other (brothers, cousins, uncles and nephews, great-grandfathers and great-grandchildren) but among whom no continued prominence according to the above rules is found. (See Diagram V)

DIAGRAM V

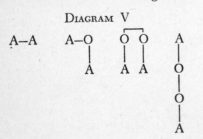

5. Lastly the data are analyzed to show the kinds of achievements by the biographees and others who are mentioned in the biographies. Five kinds of achievements are found: (1) being a member of the bureaucracy; (2) having received one or more imperial degrees; (3) being locally known for exemplary conduct, according to Confucian and other traditional ethics, such as filial piety, harmony among brothers, charity toward the public, etc.; (4) having become wealthy through commerce; and (5) being well known for distinctions in art, poetry, literature or knowledge of sacred scriptures.

The results of the analysis are given in the [table on page 45.]

A number of observations may be made on this table. First, the number of biographees among whom prominence continued for two or more generations is consistently lower in every district than the number of biographees among whom prominence did not continue after one generation. (The percentages in Column III are always smaller than those in Column IV.) This result agrees substantially with my previous study of three district histories from Chekiang Province. . . . This would seem to suggest that in these districts those who became prominent were more likely to be of unknown origin than to have come from prominent kin groups.

When we employ "being mentioned in a biography" as a criterion of prominence we find the picture slightly changes. The order is reversed so that the number of prominents in some districts "among whom prominence continued for two or more generations" became larger than those among whom prominence failed to so continue. (Some percentages in Column V are larger than those in Column VI.) . . . Expressing the same thing differently, it means that, if we lower the criterion of prominence we find a higher incidence of inbreeding among prominents. However, in every district, even with the lowered standard of prominence, "fresh blood" seems apparently to appear to the extent of 35 to 80 per cent of all cases involved in the various districts.

TABLE

Analysis / Locality	Chang Sha	Sian	Tai An	Wu Hsien
I. Total No. of Biographies	1,382	1,214	1,855	880
II. Total No. of Prominent Individuals	2,364	1,789	1,910	1,296
III. No. of Biographies among whom prominence continued for two or more generations	609 or 43%	361 or 28.8%	324 or 17.4%	364 or 41.5%
IV. No. of Biographies among whom prominence did not continue after one generation	773 or 57%	851 or 71.2%	1,531 or 82.6%	515 or 58.5%
V. No. of all prominent individuals among whom prominence continued for two or more generations	1,553 or 65%	883 or 49%	376 or 20%	755 or 58.0%
VI. No. of all prominent individuals among whom prominence did not continue after one generation	811 or 35%	906 or 51%	1,535 or 80%	541 or 42%
VII. Total number of instances of continued prominence	511	273	142	217
VIII. Number of generations through which prominence lasted among all — Two generations	237 or 46%	197 or 72%	94 or 66%	142 or 65%
Three generations	176 or 34%	46 or 16%	36 or 25%	45 or 21%
Four generations	88 or 17%	17 or 6%	9 or 6.3%	16 or 7%
Five and over	3%	6%	2.7%	7%
IX. Number of Prominent individuals who are related to the prominent lineages singly (included in V.)	20 (about 1.2% of V or 2.4% of VI)	41 (4.6% of V or 4.2% of VI)	7 (1.9% of V or 0.4% of VI)	203 (26.8% of V or 39% of VI)
X. No. of prominent individuals who are not related to prominent lineages but also are related to each other singly (included in VI)	70 (4.2% of V or 8.5% of VI)	107 (12.1% of V or 11.8% of VI)	18 (4.8% of V or 1.2% of VI)	58 (7.6% of V or 10.7% of VI)

			Chang Sha (Total XI 1553) (Total XII 811)	Sian (XI 883) (XII 906)	Tai An (XI 376) (XII 1535)	Wu Hsien (XI 755) (XII 541)
XI. Kinds of distinction achieved by all among whom prominence lasted for two or more generations	Biographees — Total 613	A*	507 or 83%	311 or 86%	267 or 82%	252 or 69%
		B	9 or 1.5%	None (Total 361)	14 or 4.6% (Total 324)	10 or 3% (Total 365)
		C	61 or 11.9%	23 or 6.3%	19 or 5.8%	45 or 13%
		D	None	None	None	None
		E	4 or 0.7%	13 or 3.7%	9 or 2.7%	38 or 10%
		F	28 or 2.9%	14 or 4%	15 or 4.9%	20 or 5%
	Non-biographees — Total 940	A	777 or 83%	422 or 81%	19 or 37%	228 or 58%
		B	81 or 8.7%	18 or 3%	18 or 35%	22 or 6%
		C	72 or 7.6% (Total 522)	70 or 13.8%	10 or 19% (Total 51)	94 or 24% (Total 390)
		D	None	None	None	1 or 0.2%
		E	7 or 0.5%	10 or 2%	4 or 7%	43 or 11%
		F	3 or 0.2%	2 or 0.2%	1 or 2%	2 or 0.8%
XII. Kinds of distinction achieved by all among whom prominence did not last after one generation	Biographees — Total 773	A	312 or 40%	494 or 58%	622 or 41%	221 or 43%
		B	72 or 9%	15 or 2%	646 or 42%	16 or 3%
		C	270 or 35% (Total 851)	277 or 27%	189 or 12% (Total 1531)	171 or 33% (Total 575)
		D	None	None	None	None
		E	20 or 2%	68 or 8%	19 or 1.2%	88 or 17%
		F	99 or 14%	47 or 5%	59 or 3.8%	19 or 4%
	Non-biographees — Total 38	A	15 or 39%	30 or 54%	None	8 or 30%
		B	17 or 44% (Total 55)	2 or 3.6%	None (Total 4)	None (Total 26)
		F	6 or 17%	23 or 42%	4 or 100%	18 or 70%

* Key to letters:
A.—Being member of the bureaucracy, or holder of any official title.
B.—Holders of imperial degrees.
C.—Exemplary conduct.
D.—Wealth through commerce.
E.—Distinctions in art, literature, calligraphy, poetry or sacred scriptures.
F.—Combinations of the above.

Next let us consider the length of continued prominence. As explained in the beginning of the paper, in each district, the number of instances of continued prominence is registered. The instances are then arranged in sequences to show through how many generations they lasted. In this section of the analysis no distinction is made between biographees and those who are merely mentioned in biographies. Two things emerge at once: (1) In all districts the incidence of prominence lasting two generations is much higher than that lasting three or more generations; and (2) in all districts the incidence of prominence lasting two or three generations constitutes 80 per cent or more of the whole. This again agrees very well with my previously obtained results in three districts of Chekiang Province. In the three Chekiang districts analyzed, the incidence of prominence lasting two to three generations constituted 75 to 94 per cent of the whole.

Two questions must be answered here. One question is, granted that prominence did not last along lineal family lines, what about individuals who became prominent because they had prominent cousins, uncles, nephews, or great-great-grandfathers? If the number of such individuals is large, does it then not mean a high degree of inbreeding among prominents?

In answering the question we must look for two kinds of facts. First, the number of prominent individuals who are related to members of prominent lineages (i.e., lineages in which prominence was continued for two or more generations) as cousins, great-great-grandfathers, nephews, etc. In three of the four district histories the number of such individuals is so small (ranging from 7 to 20) that they would be of no significant consequence to the main observations, however they are handled. . . .

A second kind of facts consist of the number of prominent individuals whose prominence was not continued lineally, but whose cousins, uncles, or brothers were prominent; the prominence of the latter was also not continued lineally. (See Diagram V.) The percentages occupied by these prominents in each district are again so small (ranging in number from 18 to 107) that they would not have made any difference, one way or the other, to the major thesis of this paper.

To sum up: the purpose of this paper is to elucidate by quantitative data the extent of vertical social mobility in Chinese society. With specifically defined criteria for the term prominence and a particular set of documentary material, it has been demonstrated that roughly 50 per cent of the local prominents in any district studied came from unknown origin and that roughly 80 per cent of the descendants beyond the grandson generation of the local prominents also became unknown.

This picture of rapid change of family fortune within a few generations is very striking, especially where class is usually determined by position in the bureaucracy, and where the position in bureaucracy depended very much upon family influence. The latter being the case, one would expect family prominence to continue, for obvious reasons. Even from the present analysis, the strength of family influence in bureaucracy is evident. For example, if we examine the biographees among whom prominence lasted for two or more generations, we find in three out of four districts over 80 per cent of them distinguished themselves by position in bureaucracy. (See Table, Column XI.) On the other hand, of the biographees among whom prominence did not last more than one generation, only about 50 per cent were bureaucrats. (See Table, Column XII.) These facts suggest that distinctions in bureaucracy had better chances of being continued along kinship lines than others. Nevertheless, taking the data as a whole, the singular thing is that, in spite of the importance of family influence, the picture of discontinued prominence emerges more vividly through this analysis than otherwise.

But here a further question arises. There is an American saying, "From shirt sleeves to shirt sleeves in three generations." Would such a saying not suggest that prominence also fails to last along lineal lines in the United States as well? While one cannot at present express a definite opinion on the subject, one must reject any close comparison between the two societies in this respect due to a basic reason. In American life an individual may achieve social prominence in a variety of ways. It has been said that the diaper service, which is now a nation-wide American industry, was started by a group of enterprising University of Chicago students during the depression. In China, on the other hand, the path of social ascension has been very narrow. Of 7,359 prominent individuals involved in 5,331 histories from four widely separated districts, only one individual was marked as distinguished due to "wealth through commerce." (See Table, Column XI, Wu Hsien.) Practically all cases of prominence in all districts were based upon (1) position in bureaucracy; (2) imperial degrees or honors; (3) distinction in literature, poetry, art, etc.; and (4) exemplary conduct following Confucian principles. The largest percentage of any group of prominents was based upon position in bureaucracy.

This being the case, the term prominence may be defined for China as we have done it here with some actual correspondence to the class structure of the society, but it becomes much more complicated if applied to the United States. Is the machine tool shop owner son of an American small town politician less prominent than his father? Where vertical mobility is complicated by so much horizontal mobility, there are as yet neither the necessary criteria nor the relevant data for drawing definite conclusions on comparative social mobility in the United States and in China.

3. FURTHER OBSERVATIONS

This picture of a fairly frequent vertical social mobility also agrees with my observations in several communities as well as in the wider Chinese national scene in general. . . .

The rather drastic difference between the conclusion offered here and that of Dr. Wittfogel, which was referred to at the beginning of this paper, is obvious. In Dr. Wittfogel's article, already mentioned, he presented a quantitative statement on the social origin of "111 leading officials" (mostly prime ministers) of T'ang dynasty and "153 biographies of officials of different rank who lived during the dynasty's middle period when T'ang institutions were in full flower." Upon analysis he found 77.5 per cent of the 111 leading officials reached their rank by way of examinations; 16.2 per cent no record; while only 6.3 per cent by way of their father's position. Among the 153 officials of different rank the picture is much less clear. Here 27.4 per cent reached officialdom by way of examination; 60.8 per cent no record; while 11.8 per cent by way of *Yin*, that is, their father's position. Dr. Wittfogel's observation is:

The number of officials in the second category who benefited from the *Yin* privilege is impressive; it is even more impressive when seen in relation to the number of degrees recorded: 18 to 42.

It is hard to see how data such as these convey any impressiveness of the *Yin* privilege. No information is given as to how the 153 officials were selected; nor what proportion of the 153 formed of the total number from which the smaller number were selected. Lastly, it is also hard to see any scientific value in any quantitative statement of which 60 per cent of the data is unknown.

Of course, Dr. Wittfogel was discussing an early period of Chinese society and the material presented here from the district histories refer mainly to later periods, especially Ming and Ch'ing dynasties. Secondly, it is probable that, with more of his monumental work coming to light, some of the present difficulties will be resolved.

After completion of this paper I discovered, to my surprise and satisfaction, that a conclusion similar to mine was reached by Dr. E. A. Kracke, Jr. in an article entitled "Family vs. Merit in Chinese Civil Service Examinations Under the Empire." Dr. Kracke's sources—two lists of civil service graduates dated 1148 and 1256—were entirely different from mine, but he came to the same general conclusion.

Bureaucratic and Non-Bureaucratic Determinants of Promotion

ROBERT M. MARSH

A sociologist who teaches at Cornell, Robert M. Marsh here raises a new question. He applies the tested "family vs. merit" formula to the promotion, rather than the recruitment, of officialdom and tries to determine the relative weight of "bureaucratic" factors (seniority, achievement) and "non-bureaucratic" factors (ethnic background, social background, etc.) in the promotion of Ch'ing civil servants.

HERETOFORE, systematic statistical studies of Ch'ing social mobility have been concerned more with one channel of bureaucratic recruitment—the examination system—than with the subsequent advancement of officials in the nine-rank (*chiu-p'in*) bureaucratic hierarchy. P'an Kuang-tan and Fei Hsiao-t'ung, Chang Chung-li, and Ho Ping-ti have dealt with the problem of the proportion of degree-holders (*chin-shih, chü-jen,* etc.) from official versus commoner families. . . .

Partly because of what we have learned from these studies of the examination competitions, but also because of what we have not learned, it is my opinion that the best strategy for future research is not to study examination lists further. There were often more degree-holders than available official posts. Even among degree-holders it may have been more difficult for commoners' sons than for the sons of official families to secure official appointment. Moreover, even after the situation obtaining in the examination competition and in the initial appointment to office has been analyzed, there remains the quite distinct problem of advancement within the bureaucracy. As we shall see, those who entered the bureaucracy through examinations did not necessarily rise higher and faster throughout their official careers than those who entered by another path. . . .

Instead of further study of examination lists, then, I propose to examine advancement within the bureaucracy itself. . . .

BUREAUCRATIC AND EXTRA-BUREAUCRATIC DETERMINANTS

What, then, were the determinants of official advancement in the Ch'ing bureaucracy? It is useful at the outset to distinguish between bureaucratic and extra-bureaucratic determinants. Something of this kind of distinction was introduced by Kracke in 1947, namely, "family versus merit," where "family" represents an extra-bureaucratic influence and "merit" a bureaucratic influence, upon success in the examination system. When the inquiry is shifted from the examination system to advancement in office, it becomes clear that other factors than merely family and merit must be included as bureaucratic and extra-bureaucratic influences. . . .

Max Weber pointed out that employ-

From Robert M. Marsh, "Bureaucratic Constraints on Nepotism in the Ch'ing Period," *Journal of Asian Studies,* XIX (1960), pp. 118–132. Reprinted by permission.

ment in a bureaucracy takes the form of a career, organized in "a system of 'promotions' according to seniority or to achievement or both." I shall treat these two factors, seniority and achievement, as the major bureaucratic determinants of advancement. It is important to realize that seniority and achievement are often in conflict. If promotions are based mainly on achievement, many officials would fail to advance very far during their careers, and outstanding young officials would assume posts above officials who were their elders. On the other hand, if seniority is more emphasized than achievement, the system of promotions would fail to motivate officials to excel in their tasks, and the bureaucracy might become a mediocre gerontocracy, with old men holding all the strategic posts. Most bureaucracies, including the Ch'ing, resort to some combination of achievement and seniority in the formal determination of advancement.

How were achievement and seniority defined in the Ch'ing bureaucracy, and what role did they play in promotion? Terms of office were normally three years for all posts. At the triennial assizes, merit ratings were drawn up for all metropolitan and provincial officials. . . . The Bureau of Records (Chi Hsün Ssu) in the Board of Civil Office kept a record of each official's seniority—his length of service in a particular bureau or organization as well as his length of service in the government as a whole. The operation of seniority is seen in the fact that the "Nomination for Promotion" list—those eligible for promotion to a given rank—usually included the names of officials whose rank during their previous term of office had been one-half rank lower. Only the officials who emerged from the assizes with a first-class recommendation, not those with a second- or third-class recommendation, were eligible for a one-half rank promotion. A first-class recommendation meant that the official had a high rating on personal conduct, ability, service record, and was not over-age or infirm. In short, one's promotion depended formally

upon achievement (conduct, ability, and service record) and upon seniority (5b rank officials were eligible for promotion to 5a rank posts, 5a to 4b, etc.).

The following offices participated in checking and cross-checking each official's record during the triennial assizes: the chief official of every civil yamen secretly submitted comments on all his subordinates to the Board of Civil Office and to the Censorate. Similar assessments of officials in the Imperial Household and of military officials were made by the Imperial Clan Court and the Censorate. After these offices had made minute inspections of the lists of nominations for promotion, the actual appointments for promotion were made centrally by the Emperor, on the basis of these lists. In practice, this was too arduous a task and only the high metropolitan and provincial officials were appointed by the Emperor himself. Officials between ranks four and seven were promoted on the recommendation of the Board of Civil Office, and those below the seventh rank were promoted directly by the departments concerned and by the Provincial authorities. . . .

To the extent, then, that Ch'ing officials' advancement was determined by (a) their achievement in office and (b) their seniority, I shall refer to their advancement as bureaucratically determined. Conversely, advancement was extra-bureaucratically determined insofar as some specific attribute of the official or some special relationship he had to others gave him preferment over other qualified officials. Among these factors were: the official's family background, his relationship to special cliques and factions from the same native place, the same class in the examination system, etc., the use of wealth for gifts, bribes, and so forth. . . .

Finally, official advancement can also be influenced by factors which, strictly speaking, are neither bureaucratic nor extra-bureaucratic per se. One of these in the Ch'ing period was the influence on advancement of the "dynastic cycle" or the "fiscal cycle" through which the dynasty and the society passed; another was the expansion and contraction of the size of the bureaucracy, i.e., the number and type of official openings. It is necessary to examine the priority of bureaucractic versus extrabureaucratic determinants of advancement before, during, and after such an expansion or contraction in the number of official posts. The fact of change in the size of the bureaucracy may or may not alter the relative influence of seniority, performance, nepotism, favoritism, and so forth. . . .

METHOD OF THE PRESENT STUDY

From the two-volume biographical dictionary, *Eminent Chinese of the Ch'ing Period (1644–1912)*, edited by Arthur W. Hummel, I drew the names of all the individuals given separate biographies who served as officials in substantive posts in the nine-rank bureaucratic hierarchy for at least two years. This gave a total of 572 officials, whose careers spanned the period from the late sixteenth century to the Revolution of 1911. The median length of career for these 572 officials was twenty-six years. Many of these officials had several years' leave during their careers, in accordance with the Confucian mourning ritual at the death of parents, or for other reasons, and these years were deducted from the total length of the career.

Eminent Chinese of the Ch'ing Period (which we shall refer to hereafter as *ECCP*) has been reviewed highly as an "outstanding achievement of American sinology," and for being "far more extensive than any other work of Chinese biography in any Western language," and "far more critical and rigorous in its use of source material than any comparable work, even in Chinese." I used it as a basis of selection because of the recency and reliability of its primary sources, its uniformly high critical standards, and its accessibility. However, it was necessary to supplement this source with extensive reference to the major biographical collections in Chinese. . . .

A major methodological problem must be confronted. These 572 officials are not a representative sample of Ch'ing officialdom. They were men who, in the informed opinion of sinological specialists, "left marks on Chinese society and obviously made history." They tend to be officials of achievement, though their achievement is not limited to their official careers. They are highly unrepresentative of a large mass of Ch'ing officials whose common attitude was "never mind seeking merit, but seek to avoid committing transgressions" (*pu ch'iu yu kung, tan ch'iu wu kuo*). Throughout this analysis, therefore, my conclusions will refer only to these 572 officials. The general validity of my findings can only be determined on the basis of future research, based upon more representative samples drawn from all Ch'ing officials, high and low, outstanding and mediocre. . . .

Having chosen a group of 572 officials to study, I next measured systematically the relative advantages and disadvantages in life which these officials derived from their family background. In doing this, I took into consideration what is known concerning the general stratification of prestige, income, authority and power during the Ch'ing period. The position of the families of these 572 officials during the generations of their fathers, grandfathers and great-grandfathers was then viewed in the perspective of this general structure of Ch'ing stratification. The family backgrounds of these 572 officials were distributed as follows:

1. Manchu families: Imperial Clansmen and Bannermen — 21%
2. Han Chinese families: Officials and Bannermen — 44%
3. Han Chinese families: degree-holders, but not officials or Bannermen — 5%
4. Han Chinese families: commoners (no officials, Bannermen or degree-holders among three previous generations of family) — 30%

100%

Chinese officials from official, Banner and degree-holding families will be combined and referred to collectively as the Chinese elite, in contrast to the remaining Chinese, those from commoner families. Of the 454 Han Chinese officials thirty-seven per cent were from commoner families and sixty-three per cent from elite families. . . .

There is a disproportionate number of high officials: fifty-two per cent of these 572 officials rose to first-rank posts, such as Grand Secretary, Presidents of the Boards and Courts, and of the Censorate. Fully seventy-six per cent of these 572 officials reached posts in the highest three ranks, at the height of their careers. Only twenty-four per cent of the total group never rose above rank four posts during their careers. This distribution is obviously an inversion of the actual pyramidal structure of the Chinese bureaucracy, in which there were fewer officials in high ranks than in lower ranks. . . .

The method chosen for the measurement of variations in official advancement was to ascertain first the highest rank within the nine-rank civil or military hierarchy which each official reached during his career, and second, the number of years he held posts in specific rank. . . .

The use of rank as the measure of official advancement is justified . . . by the fact that a movement from, say, rank 5b to 5a, or from 4a to 3b, was regarded by all as a promotion. The highest reward for an official after the triennial assizes was a promotion, and, without a special imperial edict, this was typically of one half rank at a time. "One full rank at a time would immediately become the gossip of the mandarin circle. . . . . The Government was jealously strict as to this rule: their favorite way of getting around it was, not to make big jumps, but to take little jumps with extremely great frequency." In this sense, then, we have a valid, as well as highly objective, measure of Ch'ing bureaucratic advancement.

FAMILY, SENIORITY AND OFFICIAL ADVANCEMENT

Because the Manchus were the ruling group during the Ch'ing period, and because so many of the 118 Manchu officials in the *ECCP* were Imperial Clansmen or members of highly placed Banner families, the Manchus were more likely to reach high posts than Chinese either from elite families or commoner families. Among the Manchus, eighty-four per cent rose to first-rank posts, in comparison to only forty-four per cent and forty-three per cent of the Chinese from elite and from commoner families, respectively. In fact, all but three per cent of the Manchus rose to posts above the fourth rank, whereas thirty per cent of the Chinese from elite families and twenty-nine per cent of the Chinese from commoner families did not rise above the fourth rank. . . .

It should be clear from the foregoing that there is no significant difference between the advancement of Chinese from elite families and that of Chinese from commoner families. Once commoners' sons overcame the enormous obstacles they faced in becoming an official in the first place, they appear to have reached high posts about as often as did Chinese from much more privileged elite families.[1] With respect to the length of time in high rank posts, on the other hand, Chinese from elite families outdistanced Chinese from commoner families. Chinese from elite families held first rank posts three years longer, on the average, than Chinese from commoner families (ten years vs. seven years); they held posts in the three highest ranks nine years longer, on the average, than Chinese from commoner families (twenty-seven years vs. eighteen years).

[1] To cite a parallel finding from modern American society: the children of professional and semi-professional men are much more likely to enter college than the children of laborers, but they are not significantly more likely than laborers' children to graduate from college. In both the American and the Chinese case, recruitment in the first place seems to be more influenced by family background than is success after original recruitment.

Manchus, as would be expected from what has already been said, held high rank posts considerably longer than both groups of Chinese—thirty-five years in rank one through three posts and twenty-one years in rank one posts, on the average.

Our first conclusion, then, is that family background does appear to have been a determinant of official advancement: Manchus were most likely, Chinese from elite families next most likely, and Chinese from commoner families least likely, to have long incumbency in the higher ranks. . . .

What was the influence of family background, not on advancement, but on the amount of seniority an official accumulated? Manchus were able to accumulate only slightly more seniority than Chinese from elite families. Similarly, Chinese from elite families were able to accumulate somewhat more seniority during their careers than Chinese from commoner families. Of the Manchus, fifty-two per cent had careers lasting thirty years or longer, in comparison to forty-three per cent of the Chinese from elite families and thirty-three per cent of the Chinese from commoner families. But this is not a statistically significant difference and our second conclusion is that these officials did not accumulate significantly different amounts of seniority, as a result of differences in family background among Manchus, Chinese from elite families and Chinese from commoner families.

This finding may strike some as surprising. Did not officials' sons tend to enter officialdom at a younger age than commoners' sons, and thus accumulate more seniority? This was not found to be true. For one thing, of those who received the *chin-shih* degree, the sons of elite families were not significantly younger than the sons of commoner families. Also, many of the commoners with the greatest official advancement did not rise through the examination system, but instead rose through the ranks, in the military bureaucracy. The numerous military campaigns during the Ch'ing period provided opportunities for commoners to rise through the ranks in the military

bureaucracy and thus circumvent the expensive and time-consuming process of studying for and taking the several degrees in the examination system. In this way, commoners' sons got an early start in their official careers and were able to build up almost as much seniority as the sons of official-elite families. . . .

The third point to be considered is the effect of seniority upon official advancement. . . . If we arbitrarily divide these 572 officials into four seniority groups— those whose total career lasted either between two and fifteen years, sixteen to twenty-nine years, thirty to forty-three years, or over forty-three years—we observe that seniority had a very marked effect upon both how high a man rose and also upon the length of time a man spent in specified ranks.

. . . This means that the longer an official served in the bureaucracy, the more likely he was to reach high rank posts. For example, only twenty-four per cent of those whose careers lasted less than sixteen years were able to rise to first-rank posts, in contrast to forty-two per cent of those with between sixteen and twenty-nine years' total seniority, seventy-one per cent of the group whose careers lasted between thirty and forty-three years, and fully eighty-eight per cent of those officials who accumulated the greatest seniority, i.e., over forty-three years. Again, while those officials in the two to fifteen year seniority group averaged only five years in posts in the highest three ranks, the sixteen to twenty-nine year seniority group averaged ten years, the thirty to forty-three year seniority group twenty-three years, and the over forty-three year seniority group thirty-nine years in rank one through three posts. . . .

I have shown that both family background and seniority influenced official advancement, but that family background did not significantly influence the amount of seniority officials accumulated. The next question is, did family background and seniority have an equal effect on advancement, or was one more of a determinant of advancement than the other? It may strike some readers as laboring the obvious to state that the longer an official was in office, the longer he would be in high posts. What is not self-evident, however, is whether this close relationship between seniority and advancement was equally true of Chinese from elite and from commoner families. Insofar as the formal rules of promotion in the Ch'ing bureaucracy were operative, it would appear that officials from elite and from commoner families had equal chances of advancement. But several students of the traditional Chinese bureaucracy, whom we shall cite below, are of the opinion that nepotism was rampant and that officials from commoner families therefore were not as likely to rise as officials from elite families with the same degree of seniority. According to Ch'ing statutes, officials of equal seniority and equal merit would tend to have an equal advancement; according to the nepotism argument, despite equal seniority and merit, officials from elite families would have greater advancement than officials from commoner families. What light do my data shed on this issue?

. . . The Chinese from commoner families advanced to the same extent as the Chinese from elite families, providing they had the same amount of seniority. Among Manchus, on the other hand, there is no longer a significant relationship between seniority and advancement.

This means that among Manchus, both seniority and advancement were a result of the high position their families held as Imperial Clansmen and Bannermen. Advancement among Chinese officials on the other hand, was more a result of the seniority they accumulated than of their family background. A Manchu tended to be a high official whether or not he accumulated considerable seniority; among Chinese officials, however, those most likely to be high officials tended to be those with the most seniority, whether they were from elite or from commoner families.

This same relationship can be seen in my most discriminating measure of official advancement, the length of time high-rank posts were held. I have noted that Chinese from official families held posts in the highest three ranks *nine* years longer, on the average, than Chinese from commoner families. This difference in incumbency is now sharply reduced by the factor of seniority.

Among officials with the shortest careers (less than sixteen years), Chinese from official families held posts in the three highest ranks five years longer, on the average, than Chinese from commoner families, instead of nine years longer. For officials with more seniority—sixteen to twenty-nine years and thirty to forty-three years—this difference in average incumbency in high-rank posts was further reduced, to only one year and two years, respectively. Finally, of those officials with more than forty-three years' seniority, Chinese from commoner families actually reversed the tables and held high-rank posts three years longer, on the average (thirty-six years vs. thirty-three years), than Chinese from official families.

Average Number of Years in Rank 1–3 Posts for	Total Length of Career in Years			
	2–15	16–29	30–43	44 & Over
Chinese from elite families	9	10	20	33
Chinese from commoner families	4	9	18	36
Difference in incumbency	+5	+1	+2	−3

The striking thing about this finding, in addition to the fact that it shows seniority to be a more important determinant of advancement than family background, is that one can clearly observe the slow but cumulative process by which Chinese from commoner families began their careers under a considerable handicap in comparison with Chinese from elite families, but then steadily caught up with and even outdistanced Chinese officials from elite families. Thus, seniority is seen to work significantly in favor of Chinese officials from less-privileged (commoner) families. The more seniority they accumulated, the more likely were Chinese from commoner families to catch up with and even outdistance Chinese from elite families, with respect to incumbency in high-rank posts.

The objection may be raised that, while these data on seniority may argue against nepotism, they do not necessarily eliminate the possibility of other forms of favoritism. That is, due to seniority, men with official family connections did not have a great advantage over commoners' sons within the bureaucracy. But favoritism may have operated along non-kinship lines, and in this form it may have been beyond the control of the seniority principle. It is known that high officials could recommend (*pao-chü*) lower officials as having great talent, and could request the Emperor to give these subordinates more responsibilities and to promote them. Was this practice abused in such a way that promotions were determined more by favoritism than by merit or seniority? There is reason to believe that favoritism did not operate strongly, at least not through recommendation, during the Ch'ing period. In the first place, a recommendation had to be accompanied by an explicit statement concerning whether the candidate had influential relatives, men from the same native place, etc., in the bureaucracy. Secondly, recommendation on the basis of pure favoritism was held in check by the fact that if the candidate subsequently violated bureaucratic rules, the punishment would befall the official who had recommended him.

CONCLUSION

Statistical and historical data on 572 officials suggest that in the Ch'ing bureaucracy the rule of seniority and other norms operated in such a way as to equalize the chances for advancement of officials from family backgrounds as disparate in privilege as official families and commoner families. Although the vast majority of commoners' sons never became officials, those who did enter officialdom were able to achieve about the same degree of advancement as the sons of official families and the families of the local elite, providing that they had the same amount of seniority. One way in which commoners' sons in the military bureaucracy realized even more rapid advancement than would come by seniority was the coincidence of their career with the great military campaigns of the Ch'ing period, especially the Manchu-Ming struggle for supremacy in the seventeenth century and the Taiping rebellion. If a military official scored a victory in these crucial campaigns, he tended to be rapidly promoted, despite his lack of seniority, and whether or not he was the son of an official family.

These conclusions are offered as hypotheses to be tested in future research, using more representative samples of Ch'ing officialdom. The best source for this future research is the Official Directories titled *T'ung Kuan Lu*, for various years, provinces, and so forth. These contain information on family background, education and method of entering the bureaucracy, and subsequent career for individuals serving in posts in a given province in a given year. The writer has already undertaken the analysis of several of these directories, drawn from the late eighteenth and nineteenth centuries. If the results of this further study support the present findings, we shall have a much firmer basis for asserting that bureaucratic factors such as seniority

were more important than extra-bureaucratic factors such as family background, in
determining official advancement under
the Empire. On the other hand, future
research may show that extra-bureaucratic
determinants were more significant than
the formal, impersonal, universal bureaucratic rules specified in the several editions
of the *Ta Ch'ing Hui Tien* and elsewhere.
In that event, we shall have clearer knowledge of the limitations of sources like *Eminent Chinese of the Ch'ing Period* for the

study of social mobility and bureaucratic
advancement.[1]

[1] Professor Marsh has recently published the
findings of this study. He has worked with a
sample of just over 1,000 Chinese officials, mainly
from the mid-nineteenth century. He has added
the factor of "purchase of office" among the "non-
bureaucratic" determinants and otherwise pro-
ceeds much as in the article above. He concludes:
"In the case of nineteenth-century China, advancement was determined somewhat more by
extra-bureaucratic than by bureaucratic factors."
See "Formal Organization and Promotion in a
Pre-industrial Society," *American Sociological Review*, 26 (1961), 547–556. [Editor's note]

RECRUITMENT AND THE STRUGGLE FOR POWER

The Struggle of Monarch and Nobility: Origin of the Career Open to Talent

MAX WEBER

The great German sociologist Max Weber (1864–1920) has touched on matters Chinese in several of his works. While not a trained sinologist, he had access to Chinese materials in translation and to Western works of scholarship of the early part of our century. Though some details of Weber's documentation and analysis need revision in the light of later scholarship, students of China have found his insight into the nature of bureaucracy and into the relations between society and religion provocative. In several instances, Weber's generalizations have been confirmed by recent research.

Weber's emphasis on Chinese absolutism and on the high turn-over in the civil service as a buttress of that absolutism, has received attention in recent years when the reestablishment of absolutist rule on the Chinese mainland has reopened questions about the continuity of "despotism" in the Chinese political tradition.

Weber's analysis of Chinese institutions did not become available in English until after World War II and his views have only recently begun to influence the debate on the Chinese Civil Service.

THE LITERATI

For twelve centuries social rank in China has been determined more by qualification for office than by wealth. This qualification, in turn, has been determined by education, and especially by examinations. China has made literary education the yardstick of social prestige in the most exclusive fashion. . . .

It is significant that the stratum of literati in China, although developed from ritual training, grew out of an education for genteel *laymen*. . . . In China, the literati go back, at least in the main, to the descendants, probably the younger sons, of feudal families who had acquired a literary education, especially the knowledge of writing, and whose social position rested upon this knowledge of writing and of literature. A plebeian could also acquire a knowledge of writing, although, considering the Chinese system of writing, it was difficult. But if the plebeian succeeded, he shared the prestige of any other scholar. Even in the feudal period, the stratum of literati was not hereditary or exclusive. . . .

Apart from knowledge of scriptures as a means of discerning tradition, a knowledge of the calendar and of the stars was required for discerning the heavenly will and, above all, for knowing the *dies fasti* and *nefasti* [auspicious and inauspicious

Reprinted by permission of Oxford University Press, Inc. from Max Weber, *From Max Weber: Essays in Sociology*, translated and edited by Hans H. Gerth and C. Wright Mills, Oxford University Press, New York, 1946, pp. 416–420, 423–426.

days], and it seems that the position of the literati has also evolved from the dignified role of the court astrologer. . . .

If one may trust the Annals, the literati, being adherents of the bureaucratic organization of the state as a compulsory institution, were opponents of feudalism from the very beginning. This is quite understandable because, from the standpoint of their interests, the administrators should be only men who were personally qualified by a literary education. . . .

The close relation of the literati to princely service came about during the struggle of the prince with the feudal powers. . . .

The relation of the Chinese literati to princely service as the normal source of income differentiated them as a status group from the philosophers of Antiquity and from at least the educated laymen of India, who, in the main, were socially anchored in fields remote from any office. As a rule, the Chinese literati strove for princely service both as a source of income and as a normal field of activity. Confucius, like Lao-tzu, was an official before he lived as a teacher and writer without attachment to office. We shall see that this relation to state-office (or office in a "church state") was of fundamental importance for the nature of the mentality of this stratum. For this orientation became increasingly important and exclusive. The opportunities of the princes to compete for the literati ceased to exist in the unified empire [221 B.C. on]. The literati and their disciples then came to compete for the existing offices, and this development could not fail to result in a unified orthodox doctrine adjusted to the situation. This doctrine was to be *Confucianism*. . . .

THE DEVELOPMENT OF THE EXAMINATION SYSTEM

. . . In the Confucian period (sixth to to fifth century B.C.) the possibility of ascent into official positions as well as the system of examinations was still unknown. It appears that, as a rule, at least in the feudal states, the "great families" were in the possession of power. It was not until the Han dynasty—which was established by a parvenu—that the bestowal of offices according to merit was raised to the level of a principle. And not until the T'ang dynasty, in 690 A.D., were regulations set up for the highest degree. As we have already mentioned, it is highly probable that literary education, perhaps with a few exceptions, was at first actually, and perhaps also legally, monopolized by the "great families." . . . Vestiges of this continued to the end. Members of the imperial clan, although not freed from all examinations, were freed from examination for the first degree. And the trustees, whom every candidate for examinations, until recently, had to name, had to testify to the candidate's "good family background." During modern times this testimony has only meant the exclusion of descendants of barbers, bailiffs, musicians, janitors, carriers, and others. Yet alongside this exclusion there was the institution of "candidates for the mandarinate"; that is, the descendants of mandarins enjoyed a special and preferred position in fixing the maximum quota of examination candidates from each province. The promotion lists used the official formula "from a mandarin family and from the people." The sons of well-deserved officials held the lowest degree as a title of honor. All of which represent residues of ancient conditions.

The examination system has been fully carried through since the end of the seventh century. This system was one of the means the patrimonial[1] ruler used in preventing the formation of a closed estate, which, in the manner of feudal vassals and office nobles, would have monopolized the

[1] In his sociology of types of authority, Weber had defined: "Where authority is primarily oriented to tradition but in its exercise makes the claim of full personal powers, it will be called 'patrimonial' authority." It is to this category that Weber assigns the Chinese monarchy. See Weber, *The Theory of Social and Economic Organization*, Free Press, Glencoe, Ill., 1947, p. 347. [Editor's note]

rights to the office prebends.[2] The first traces of the examination system *seem* to emerge about the time of Confucius (and Huang K'an) in the sub-state of Ch'in, a locality which later became autocratic. The selection of candidates was determined essentially by military merit. Yet, even the *Li Chi* and the *Chou Li* demand, in a quite rationalist way, that the district chiefs examine their lower officials periodically with regard to their morals, and then propose to the emperor which of them should be promoted. In the unified state of the Han Emperors, pacifism began to direct the selection of officials. The power of the literati was tremendously consolidated after they had succeeded in elevating the correct Kuang Wu to the throne in 21 A.D. and in maintaining him against the popular "usurper" Wang Mang. During the struggle for prebends, which raged during the following period, . . . the literati developed into a unified *status group*.

. . . The T'ang dynasty, for the first time, regulated the literati's position and established colleges for their education (in the seventh century). It also created the *Han lin Yüan*, the so-called "academy," which first edited the Annals in order to gain precedents, and then controlled the emperor's correct deportment. Finally, after the Mongol storms, the national Ming dynasty in the fourteenth century decreed statutes which, in essence, were definitive. Schools were to be set up in every village, one for every twenty-five families. As the schools were not subsidized, the decree remained a dead letter. . . . Officials selected the best pupils and enrolled a certain number in the colleges. In the main, these colleges have decayed, although in part they have been newly founded. In 1382,

[2] Another of Weber's special terms, used to describe certain "modes of support" of the patrimonial ruler's retainer. "Prebends" can consist of allowances of goods or money from the ruler's store; rights of use of land in return for service, or appropriated property income, fees, or taxes. See *ibid.*, p. 351. Weber reserves the term *salary* for the remuneration of administrators in a bureaucracy, a sub-type of the "legal-rational" form of authority. [Editor's note]

prebends in the form of rice rents were set aside for the "students." In 1393, the number of students was fixed. After 1370, only examined men had claims to offices. . . .

At once a fight set in between the various regions, especially between the North and the South. The South even then supplied candidates for examinations who were more cultured, having experienced a more comprehensive environment. But the North was the military foundation stone of the empire. Hence the emperor intervened and *punished* (!) the examiners who had given the "first place" to a Southerner. Separate lists for the North and the South were set up, and moreover, a struggle for the patronage of offices began immediately. Even in 1387 special examinations were given to officers' sons. The officers and officials, however, went further, and demanded the right to designate their successors, which meant a demand for re-feudalization. In 1393 this was conceded, but in the end only in a modified form. The candidates presented were preferentially enrolled in the colleges, and prebends were to be reserved for them: in 1465 for three sons, in 1482 for one son, and in 1453 we meet with the purchase of college places, and in 1454 with the purchase of offices. During the fifteenth century, as is always the case, these developments arose from the need for military funds. In 1492 these measures were abolished, but in 1529 they were reintroduced.

The *departments* also fought against one another. The Board of Rites was in charge of the examinations after 736, but the Board of Civil Office appointed the officials. The examined candidates were not infrequently boycotted by the latter department, the former answering by going on strike during the examinations. Formally, the minister of rites, actually, the minister of offices (the major-domo) were in the end the most powerful men in China. Then merchants, who were expected to be less "stingy," came into office. Of course, this hope was quite unjustified. The Manchus favored the old traditions and thus the literati and, as far as possible, "purity" in the distribution of offices. But now, as before, three routes to office existed side by side: (1) imperial favor for the sons of the "princely" families (examination privileges); (2) easy examinations (officially every three to six years) for the lower officials by the higher officials who controlled patronage . . . ; (3) the only legal way: to qualify effectively and purely by examination.

In the main, the system of examination has actually fulfilled the functions as conceived by the emperor. . . . Both parties, emperor and graduates, had a stake in the examination system, or at least they thought they had. From the emperor's standpoint, the examination system . . . facilitated a competitive struggle for prebends and offices among the candidates, which stopped them from joining together into a feudal office nobility. Admittance to the ranks of aspirants was open to everybody who was proved to be educationally qualified. The examination system thus fulfilled its purpose.

Mobility in an Oriental Despotism

KARL A. WITTFOGEL

Karl A. Wittfogel, whose earlier article on the hereditary privilege is reprinted on pages 34–40, has attracted considerable attention in recent years with his thesis about "Oriental Despotism." An ex-Marxist, Professor Wittfogel has resurrected and fleshed out the concept of "Asiatic society" developed by the classical economists and Marx. In an "Asiatic" or "hydraulic" society, government control over vital economic functions, especially irrigation water, leads to a despotic regime where the state wields nearly total control over all aspects of society and atomizes all potentially rival social groupings. Professor Wittfogel has also acknowledged his indebtedness to Max Weber, whose ideas he has further developed.

Since Professor Wittfogel's data actually bespeak more continuity in Chinese officialdom than his general thesis allows for, the student should remember that Professor Wittfogel's generalizations about "Oriental Despotism" are based on the study of a number of societies, not just China.

[In Oriental Despotism] the autocrat has been likened to the life-giving sun, to fierce animals, and to the merciless forces of lightning, storm, and flood. To his subjects he is indeed all these, and those among them who act in his name are eager both to execute his will and to influence it.

But the master of a tool is also its servant. The autocrat depends operationally upon the persons who implement his orders. The history of Oriental courts records endless attempts to influence the autocrat and equally endless attempts by the ruler to prevail over all personal and impersonal (bureaucratic) forces. The resulting conflicts are many. . . .

. . . Since the interests of the officialdom frequently suggest one decision and the ruler's interests another, there is considerable room for conflict. Needless to say, the sovereign will prevail the more completely, the more he determines the choice of his civil and military functionaries, and the more he controls their executive procedures. . . .

The relations [between despot and officials] are always slanted in favor of the despot, and this is so even where the officials enjoy hereditary privileges. It is particularly so where the ruler appoints his officials without the need to consider a self-perpetuating (noble) bureaucracy.

. . . The despot may reduce the social homogeneity of the ranking officials by the appointment of outsiders; he may place men of lowly origin above officials of upper-class background; he may give precedence to priests, "barbarian" nobles, eunuchs, or slave officials. In the sovereign's hand such devices become the weapons for asserting his autocratic power against the will, and the unending political intrigues, of the ranking officialdom. . . .

The Chinese examination system has

From Karl A. Wittfogel, *Oriental Despotism,* Yale University Press, New Haven, 1957, pp. 343, 345–354, 363–364. Reprinted by permission.

frequently been viewed as an institution which, throughout the period of imperial rule, gave the commoners access to office. Since participation in the examinations was based not on invitation from above but on the would-be candidate's spontaneous application, the Chinese bureaucracy may well seem, during this period, to have been recruited in large part from "the people."

The Chinese examination system did in fact make it possible for a number of qualified commoners to enter the bureaucracy; but its social effects were much more modest than popular legend would have us believe. What actually did happen? The question is sufficiently important for an understanding of mobility in hydraulic society to justify a brief statement of the function—and the limitation—of the Chinese examination system.

First of all, the Chinese examination system provided the absolutist governments of China with candidates for office only during a limited and relatively late period. In Chou times and probably also under the Shang dynasty the bulk of all officials held positions because their forefathers had done so. During the Han dynasty (206 B.C.–A.D. 220) entry upon a government career depended essentially on appointment by the emperor or by a special official; in addition, office-holding fathers might recommend their own sons. The method of "recommending sons" (*jen tzu*) favored the self-perpetuation of particular families in the bureaucracy, while appointment favored the self-perpetuation of the ranking officialdom generally. An examination of the biographical data included in the dynastic histories of the Han period gives considerable insight into the effects of these procedures, which are in fact a bureaucratic variant of the aristocratic principle of cooptation. Basing ourselves on this source, we find that no more than 8 per cent of all officials of known social background were commoners, the remainder being relatives of the emperor (in the main, affinals), members of other noble families, or—and

in their great majority—the relatives of officials.

The period of disruption which ended in A.D. 589 modified earlier patterns of government. Although wars and conquest provided opportunities for the rise of social outsiders, a limited number of families were able to perpetuate their hold on the state apparatus. Under the infiltration and conquest dynasties of North China, nobles of Inner Asian origin prevailed; and in the South indigenous "hereditary families" (*shih chia*) were similarly prominent. The biographies of the Southern Chin dynasty (216–419) indicate that about 9.5 per cent of all officials with known background may have been commoners.

The much-discussed examination system was established only in the time of the reunified empire by the short-lived Sui dynasty (581–618). It was fully developed by the subsequent T'ang dynasty—that is, it came into being something like seventeen hundred years after the beginning of the Chou dynasty and eight hundred years after the beginning of the imperial era. And even during the first half of the thirteen hundred years of its existence its influence on the social composition of the imperial bureaucracy was seriously restricted by institutionalized social discrimination, by hereditary claims to office (the *yin* privilege), and, under the conquest dynasties, by the politically prominent nobles of the "barbarian" master nationality.

The Chinese examination system was established not by democratic forces but one-sidedly by a despotic ruler. The ranking officials certainly influenced the original plan; and they implemented it, once it was established. Anyone who was eligible to participate in the examinations could take the initiative in applying; and this is a significant deviation from the earlier appointment system. However, even under the examination system the emperor and his officials ultimately decided whom they would employ, and how they would employ them. The government determined in advance how many degrees would be conferred; and even the holders of the most important degree, the *chin-shih*, originally were admitted to office only after they had also passed a sort of civil service test.

The insistence upon a thorough classical education gave the members of official families—and, of course, also the relatives of the ruling house—an enormous cultural and social advantage. This advantage was enhanced by measures that, on the one hand, restricted the commoners' access to office and, on the other, provided the relatives of higher and middle officials with institutionalized claims to office.

The Sui statutes that initiated the examination system expressly excluded "artisans and merchants" from holding office. A similar policy of discrimination prevailed under the T'ang, and, with certain modifications, also under the Sung dynasty. Since commerce, more than any other occupation, provided commoners with opportunities for acquiring wealth and education, discrimination against merchants excluded from government exactly those commoners who were materially best equipped to prepare for the examinations.

Moreover, the statutes that restricted the artisans and merchants gave added advantages to the bureaucracy. On the basis of their governmental position, higher and middle officials were granted the "protective" (*yin*) privilege of having one or several of their sons enter the civil service without having to pass an examination. This privilege, which in a new guise reestablished time-honored prerogatives, emerged in the Sui and T'ang dynasties— that is, as soon as the examinations were instituted. The *yin* system underwent considerable change during the Sung period, but it continued to play a significant role at this time and also under the two first of the four great dynasties of conquest, Liao and Chin.

The Mongols were deeply suspicious of their Chinese subjects. They therefore preferred appointment for their Chinese officials to any other method of selection. During the great part of their rule the Mongols held no examinations; and when eventually the examinations were reinstituted, the number of *chin-shih* degrees remained grotesquely low: "averages totaled not more than seventy (including a number of 'barbarians')." They also restricted the number of *yin* sons and grandsons to one, as compared with ten and twenty beneficiaries under Sung rule and six under Chin rule. But they favored those who held the *yin* privilege by permitting them to enter the bureaucratic hierarchy in the fifth rank, a higher level than that granted in T'ang days. The Ming and Ch'ing emperors reduced the *yin* prerogative to a shadow of its former self. They granted it only to the descendants of higher officials; and its beneficiaries could attain high positions only if they had passed the examinations.

The role of the holders of the *chin-shih* degree indicates one crucial function of the examination system. The intensive knowledge of the Chinese classics required for the examinations saturated the students both with the social philosophy of the ruling bureaucracy and with the great traditions of its semimanagerial and absolutist statecraft. Thus the competitive examination system was an excellent means for thoroughly indoctrinating ambitious commoners and for compelling the talented sons of officials and bureaucratic gentry families to submit to a most comprehensive professional ideological training.

The examinations were open to commoners during the first six hundred years with serious restrictions, and during the last six hundred years without such hindrances. But how many commoners did actually rise to official position in the government of imperial China through this method? Again the biographies, included in each of the official dynastic histories, provide us with invaluable, if selective, information. The biographies are numerous, more numerous in fact than any other collection of corresponding data in any other agrarian civilization, and they deal essentially with high and middle officials, who are listed not because of their rank, but because of their achievements.

Our preliminary effort to determine the social background of the official biographies in some of the more important imperial dynasties indicates that during the T'ang period (618–907) some 83 per cent of all socially definable officials had an upper-class background: about 70 per cent were from the families of officials and 13 per cent from the ruling house or other noble families. Almost 7 per cent were "barbarians" (the T'ang ruling house was, at least in part, of Turkish origin). And less than 10 per cent were commoners.

The corresponding figures for the Sung dynasty (960–1279) suggest a minimum figure of some 85 per cent of officials with an upper-class background: 72 per cent descended from the families of officials and 13 per cent from the ruling house. About 15 per cent were commoners.

Our survey of the biographies of the Mongol dynasty (1234–1368) suggests that about 85 per cent of all socially definable officials had an upper-class background: 74 per cent were descended from the families of officials and 11 per cent from the ruling house. About 15 per cent were descended from commoners.

The indigenous rulers of the Ming dynasty were not at all eager to restore the pre-Mongol privileges of the bureaucracy. They controlled the officials from above through political eunuchism. And they made it easier for commoners to enter the state service by crippling the *yin* privilege and by not discriminating against artisans and merchants, as the Sui, T'ang, and Sung governments had done. Under the Ming dynasty 77 per cent of all socially definable officials had an upper-class background: 63 per cent were descended from the families of officials, 14 per cent from the ruling house. And about 23 per cent were descended from commoners.

The Manchu rulers were no more in-

clined than their Ming predecessors to favor the bureaucracy's tendency toward self-perpetuation. They controlled their Chinese officials from above through tribal nobles, whose political position was bulwarked by the preservation of their hereditary prerogatives. And they facilitated the access of commoners to examinations and office, as the Ming rulers had done, through curtailing the *yin* privilege and through not discriminating against artisans and merchants. They particularly stressed purchase of degrees as a means of preventing the *shên-shih* (the officials and degree-holders) from becoming a socially homogeneous body.

An imperial edict of 1727 expressed sharp criticism of many persons who attained office through examinations. "If the official career should be left completely to those who rise through examinations, they would just firmly join together and work for their private interest against the public interest. This is of great harm to the public welfare and to the livelihood of the people. The purchase system should be appropriately expanded."

According to a recent analysis of the social background of *chin-shih* candidates, the percentage of candidates whose forebears were neither officials nor degree-holders increased greatly during the 19th century. And a study of the 19th-century *shên-shih* reveals that persons who joined this group not through examination but through purchase of a degree constituted about 32 per cent of the "lower gentry" during the first half of the century and about 36 per cent after 1854.

The results of our analysis are confirmed for the Sung period by two lists of *chin-shih* graduates for 1148 and 1256 respectively, which, although incomplete as to social background data,[1] throw additional

---

[1] For details concerning the two lists see Kracke [above, pp. 1–8]. The second list has conspicuous gaps . . . , and both, like the dynastic biographies, provide only selected data concerning the protagonists' official background. In his thoughtful study of this background, Kracke considered only relatives in the direct line up to, and

light upon our problem. Assuming that during the thirty-year period from 1142 to 1171 almost forty-five hundred persons passed the examinations, that all these persons and an equal number who "presumably entered the service by other methods" achieved government positions, that at least one-half of all *chin-shih* graduates, as relatives of the emperor, acting officials, or members of the bureaucratic gentry, belonged to the ruling class,[2] and that the average length of office tenure was something like twenty years, we find among the thirty-three thousand civil and military officials a total of 9 per cent who may have come from the rank of commoners. These figures are well below the 15 per cent suggested by our earlier analysis. To adjust

including, the great-grandfathers . . . . However, besides such individuals the list of 1256 mentions regularly the brothers of "graduates" who held degrees or offices. In two cases, in which no direct forebears had held public office, five and seven brothers respectively did so. And both lists note brothers, uncles, granduncles, and great-great grandfathers whenever they are family heads. Differing from Kracke, we view graduates with such relatives as having an official background; and in consequence we add sixteen more cases for 1148 and twenty more for 1256 to his graduates with official background. This raises the percentages of graduates with known official background from 42.1 to 45.6 per cent in the first case and from 43.7 to 49.5 per cent in the second.

[2] In his 1947 study, Dr. Kracke distinguishes essentially between graduates with and without an official background. Our figures, therefore, can be expected to be somewhat larger than his. All graduates of 1148 who are members of the imperial family, Chao, are listed in the Sung account as having relatives who held official position; and they are therefore included by Dr. Kracke. However, in the 1256 record only the names of the Chao graduates, who numbered twenty-seven, are listed. Dr. Kracke is consistent in not including them; but we are equally consistent in doing so. We thus find that 50.3 per cent of all graduates of 1256 belonged to the ruling class. In view of the limited character of the background data contained in both lists, our above estimate that "at least one half of all *chin-shih* graduates . . . belonged to the ruling class" is probably a conservative one. I should like to take this opportunity to thank Mr. Fang Chao-ying for calling my attention to the imperial relatives mentioned in the lists and Professor Tung-tsu Chu for his careful reexamination of the social data contained in the two Sung lists.

them, we would have to assume that the Sung emperor appointed more than the above-suggested number of commoners without benefit of a degree.

Many details of the Chinese examination system still need clarification, but this much seems certain: if the Sui and T'ang emperors established the examination system, in part at least, in order to alter the social composition of the ranking officialdom, then it must be said that the system failed to achieve this purpose. The examinations provided the ambitious core of the ruling class with a most intensive intellectual and doctrinal training; and they added a varying amount of "fresh blood" to the ranking officialdom. But they did not destroy the trend toward sociopolitical self-perpetuation which dominated the thoughts and actions of this group. . . .

In open and property-based societies a commoner may rise above his original station, either through political or economic achievement. Members of the upper class may try to prevent his ascent, but they cannot forbid it. They may discriminate against the power *parvenu* or the *nouveau riche* personally, but usually the newcomer's children or grand-children achieve social acceptance. This was the general pattern in the democratic city-states of ancient Greece. And it is increasingly typical for such modern industrial countries as England, Scandinavia, Australia, and the United States.

This pattern of democratic and spontaneous social mobility differs fundamentally from the patterns of social mobility that characterize hydraulic society. In hydraulic society, the lowly ones who entered the ruling class rarely came from the ranks of the free and prominent commoners. In China the number of persons who could obtain a higher examination degree was carefully restricted; and even this Chinese pattern was by no means typical for the majority of all Oriental civilizations. . . .

Members of [commoner] groups rose to positions of distinction not because they overcame barriers of established wealth and power through their own efforts, but because the ruler was sufficiently strong to select whom he pleased and to place the person of his choice where he pleased. What vertical mobility there was in hydraulic society resulted from manipulation from above.

Region, Family, and Individual
in the Examination System

E. A. KRACKE, JR.

In this article, Professor Kracke examines different applications of the ideal
of free access to office for the men of talent. He reminds us that the civil
service and its recruitment procedures functioned in a political context which
often shaped the manner in which political ideals were applied.

THE traditional Chinese examination system occupies a central place in Chinese political theory and in the practical structure of Chinese society and was one of the earliest of Chinese institutions to attract the attention and inspire the imagination of Western political thinkers. It has symbolized dramatically the ideal of a public career open to all in the measure of their worth and ability. Yet the relation between the ideal and the reality of the examinations remains in some ways elusive. . . . The continued appeal to early statements and precedents has somewhat deceptively cloaked changes in function, and the resulting shifts in relation between ideal and reality have inevitably modified the real meaning of the ideals within Chinese thought. To understand the real meaning of the examinations in Chinese political thought, therefore, it is necessary to trace the change in their actual practice over the centuries. The present study is concerned with a single aspect of this change—the variation in interpreting the concept of free opportunity and the differing results of this for the several regions of the empire.

1. THE IDEAL OF FREE OPPORTUNITY AND ITS REALIZATION

Behind the concept of competitive examinations for office lies the ideal of Confucius that only ability and virtue qualify a man for service in government—an ideal inherited by such divergent Confucian schools as that of Hsün-tzu, authoritarian in its trend, and that of Mencius, whose more liberal principles predominated in Chinese thought from the T'ang dynasty onward. Since the more favored Confucian doctrine held that human nature (including the mind) was inherently capable of perfection, it followed that ability and virtue were independent of the status into which one might be born. Therefore the means should be provided, and the way left open, for any man to rise from low birth-status to the highest rank.

We must not read into this concept certain connotations apt to accompany it in the Occident. In Confucian theory, once

Reprinted from E. A. Kracke, Jr., "Region, Family, and Individual in the Chinese Examination System," in John K. Fairbank, ed., *Chinese Thought and Institutions*, University of Chicago Press, Chicago, 1957, pp. 251–268. Reprinted by permission of the University of Chicago Press. Copyright © 1957 by Robert Redfield. [Besides the omitted text passages indicated by asterisks, four statistical tables have also been omitted for the sake of brevity.]

men's character and status were established, their differing needs and moral attainments made it natural that they should receive differing material advantages, prerogatives, responsibilities, and liberties. Certain occupations—including in earlier periods commerce and handicrafts—brought ethical disqualification for an official career. Freedom of opportunity to develop one's abilities, in short, was quite compatible with strong class distinction. To the Chinese thinker this was not inconsistent. To him the need of society took priority over the will of the individual. It was a man's duty, rather than his right, to place his services at the ruler's disposal; he should accept office but not seek it.

Practical conditions at all times modified the operation of the theory, however. On one hand, although universal education would seem to follow logically from Confucian political doctrines, the creation of schools and the support of students on such a scale were scarcely conceivable with the material resources available to traditional Chinese society in the best of times. Diversity in economic development, increasing the disparity of educational resources among groups and places, necessarily made opportunity more unequal. Differences in examination methods and requirements also favored some groups and places over others. On the other hand, the educated Chinese in normal times sought office, whether as his right or as his duty, almost as eagerly as his occidental counterpart. Since in most periods no other career could rival the prestige offered by the civil service, the examinations, which gradually became the preeminently honored gateway to the service, assumed a unique importance. Above all other ways of entrance, they represented the principle of recruitment through merit. But they never quite won either an exclusive control of the recruitment process or unchallenged approval as an ideal. Testing ability rather than character, they failed to satisfy some of the more zealous Confucians, and they were always obliged to compete with other recruitment methods such

as recommendation, protection (yin-pu), promotion from the clerical service, or sale of official rank. The changing balance among methods was of course intimately involved with the political movements of different periods. The honor accorded to the examination system, its practical importance, and the zeal and honesty of its administration saw successive periods of rise and decline. While the story of the examinations reflected in some degree the history of social mobility in the bureaucracy as a whole, the reflection was never complete.

The length of the present study permits only brief and inadequate reference to most of the factors mentioned above. Primary emphasis will be placed on discernible relationships between available data of three kinds: population concentrations and changes, regional representation among examination graduates, and regional patterns of vertical social mobility among the graduates. The focus in time will be on the period from the mid-seventh century A.D. to the end of the nineteenth, with somewhat greater attention to the earlier periods when competition in the examinations was free from regional limitations. It is scarcely necessary to emphasize that explanations of the examination system based on investigations thus limited in scale and scope can arrive only at partial and tentative conclusions. These are presented in the hope of contributing toward the fuller study that is needed.

2. REGIONAL REPRESENTATION UNDER FREE INTERREGIONAL COMPETITION, 655–1279

The examinations were at first, in the Han dynasty, primarily a method of classifying candidates who had been recommended for governmental service. They were slow to assume the role of a major recruitment method, and during earlier centuries the numbers who passed annually were rather few. Even during the earlier reigns of the T'ang dynasty, before 655, there seem never to have been more than twenty-five men so selected in any single year; the annual average during this time was less than nine men. (Because of irregularities in the spacing of examinations, both before and after the triennial rule was adopted in 1067, the annual *average* of graduates during a period of years, including the years between examinations, is the only practical unit for comparison.) The first significant increase came abruptly with the rise to power of the ambitious empress Wu Tse-t'ien. Her sharp eye discerned in the technique of examination, it seems, a tool for her projected usurpation of power. It might serve to tap the heretofore neglected source of trained men in the Southeast and help to dislodge from power the tightly knit clique from the capital region, which was devoted to the interests of the reigning dynasty. In 655 she caused forty-four doctoral examination degrees to be conferred, and, in a seven-year period before the proclamation of her new dynasty, the annual average exceeded fifty-eight men. She thus, perhaps unintentionally, established the quantitative importance of examinations for recruitment. At the same time, by the favored treatment of the graduates, she enhanced the prestige of the new method as the accepted channel to power. The process of opening opportunities to wider groups had begun.

After the fall of Empress Wu, the restored T'ang rulers employed the same tool and, for a brief time, raised still higher the annual average of degrees conferred. The disorders of the later T'ang and of the succeeding Five Dynasties period (907–60) brought a hiatus in the growth of the system, and practices that facilitated favoritism in examination-grading restricted the opportunity of men who were without influential connections. At the end of the tenth century, however, the Sung rulers, who had now reconstituted the empire, took new steps to develop the system. They instituted a series of measures to insure the greatest possible objectivity in grading the examination papers. Simultaneously, they expanded the number of degrees annually awarded until these more than dou-

bled the highest T'ang averages. The numbers of degrees remained high during most of the remaining years of the dynasty for which we have statistics. Usually around two hundred or more per annum, at times they averaged nearly two hundred and forty.

In using the examination technique to further her plans for usurpation, Empress Wu had not only opened a governmental career to wider groups. By bringing in new men from the Southeast to compete with those of the capital region, she had also consciously or unconsciously created a situation that would continue to strengthen the imperial position through the balancing of potentially rival regional groups within the bureaucracy. Equitable recruitment of officials from all areas also offered advantages beyond this: it might strengthen the allegiance of well-represented regions and avoid the antagonism of frustrated literati; it might insure that interests of all regions would find a voice in government councils; it might encourage the development of an educated local leadership to assist the centrally appointed regional officials. It is hard to say how far rulers or officials were aware of these advantages. There is ample evidence that regional feeling was strong in the civil service, and any inequities in recruitment were fully noticed. We see this in the discussion of the subject between Ssu-ma Kuang and Ou-yang Hsiu in the eleventh century. Regional inequality still existed, but its patterns were now quite different from those of five centuries before, as we may see from figures preserved in a memorial of Ssu-ma Kuang. These figures concern the distribution of both the competing and the successful candidates for the degree of doctor of letters (*chin-shih*) in the years 1036, 1038, and 1040. They represent scattered illustrative examples, from varying circuits for different years, but their trend is surprisingly clear. The area of the capital [K'aifeng] produced, in all the years named, between 170 and 270 doctors of letters for each million households of its population.

But the areas along the North border, those in the Southwest (excepting the vicinity of Chengtu in modern Szechwan), and the South Central area produced, in the examples given, roughly one to four such graduates per million households. No figures are given for the remaining seven circuits in the flourishing East Central and Southeast areas, but at a conservative estimate these must have supplied close to twelve per million households, several times the ratio of the rest of the empire, excluding the capital. While these seven circuits held somewhat over half the empire's population, they included a much smaller proportion of its territory; among them were the densely populated areas of the Szechwan Basin, on the west, and the fertile Yangtze delta. It may be particularly significant that they held many of the empire's greatest cities, including the trade emporia of the southeastern coast. Ou-yang Hsiu's discussion of the subject makes clear that the Southeast already rivaled the capital as a cultural center and dominated the examinations to a degree that incurred the envy of other parts of China.

The significance of these facts becomes clearer in the light of fuller statistics derived from lists of graduates for two later Sung examinations. Two examinations, out of more than a hundred held during the Sung period, afford a slender basis for generalization, but the particular selection (made by chance preservation) is a rather fortunate one. The two examinations—one of 1148 and one of 1256—came near the beginning and near the end, respectively, of the era during which the Sung rulers reigned at Hangchow, after most of North China had fallen to the Jurchen invaders in 1127. During the years immediately following the northern debacle, much of South China was also ravaged by Jurchen raids, but with the return of peace after 1141 the administrative system was largely restored to order. The following century was relatively undisturbed, and Sung culture flourished despite the persistence of serious economic problems until after 1233,

when a new threat appeared in the North. The Mongols raided Szechwan in 1253 and invaded it more seriously in 1258. Fifteen years later the main Sung defenses were breached and the remaining Chinese resisters driven to the mountains and seas. The examination of 1148 thus fell in a time of peace following disorder, and that of 1256 at the threshold of disorder after long peace. Where the graduate lists of the two examinations agree in their testimony concerning Chinese society, it is not improbable that they typify the intervening century as well; and, since they are relatively complete, they supply an invaluable cross-section of the successful candidates in their respective years.

Among the most striking parallels between the two lists is their indication of the dominant place held by the regions with denser population, larger numbers of great cities, and more advanced commercial development. Among the sixteen circuits of the empire at that time, the two southeastern coastal circuits, Fu-chien and Che-tung, containing the outstanding commercial cities of the age, stand out above all others, supplying together more than 40 per cent of the empire's total in both years. The share of the empire's graduates that came from these circuits was even greater than their share of the empire's population; in both years they were far ahead of all other circuits in numbers of graduates per million households.

In other circuits the correlation between a dense population and a high ratio of graduates to population is less consistent, perhaps because the smaller numbers of graduates permitted greater accidental fluctuations, or because of factors outside of our present consideration. But such a correlation is still strongly suggested. And when we compare evidence on the relative urban development of the several circuits, we find again that a greater number of large prefectures tends to be associated with more degrees per capita.

Clearly the disparity in representation between the border regions and the central, noted by Ssu-ma Kuang in the eleventh century, still existed in the twelfth and thirteenth. The large proportion of unsuccessful candidates from the border areas, seen in the eleventh century, was surely not accidental. As Ou-yang Hsiu had then pointed out, the greater chance for success enjoyed by each candidate from the more populated regions reflected the more rigorous selective process through which he had qualified in the preliminary local tests. But the situation was now modified in two respects. The region of the new Southern Sung capital (at Hangchow in Che hsi) was extremely modest in its share of the degrees as compared with the old Northern Sung capital at K'ai-feng. And the men of four southwestern circuits appear to have progressed very significantly in their ability to compete with candidates from the more developed areas. There is evidence that a natural process of regional equalization was under way, apparently without resort to any formal action toward this end.

3. SOCIAL GROUP REPRESENTATION UNDER FREE INTERREGIONAL COMPETITION

Beyond indicating the local distribution of the successful candidates, the Sung examination lists give us in most cases little specific indication of their social background. Only one group is clearly singled out—that of the graduates who traced their descent to the founder of the Sung dynasty or his house. . . .

For the candidates other than the imperial descendants, the two lists are less specific. But they do supply important clues to the relative numbers of candidates descended from officials and of those without such ancestry. They state regularly the offices held in the candidates' direct paternal line for the three previous generations, and in 1148 also specify the absence of such offices. Data on collateral relatives are unfortunately lacking or too sporadic for comparative purposes, but the completeness of the data on the direct paternal line makes it possible to use them as a yardstick for comparing the degree of official-family

influence in different periods and areas. The variations of such influence that appear in this limited category of information may reflect with reasonable accuracy the variations of official-family background in a more general sense. For the sake of convenience, we may refer to the graduates who had officials in the three direct generations of their paternal ancestry as "officially-connected men," and those with no such indications as "new men," remembering that these terms are used in this restricted sense only.

Having in common only the negative quality of nonofficial paternal ancestry, the "new men" with whom we have to do were certainly not a homogeneous group. Apart from the fact, already noted, that some of our "new men" had or may have had officials among their relatives in collateral lines, other incomplete data indicate, as we might expect, that a number of them came from families with a past tradition of education. Some had forebears who had passed examinations, although they do not seem to have held office. Some had brothers, or in one case a nephew, who had passed examinations or held office—suggesting, though not conclusively, a family background of education. Recorded instances of relatives with degrees are, however, few and scattered and serve only to suggest that the line separating the officially-connected from the outsiders may have been a rather shadowy one at this period.

The regional variations in the proportion of new men are much more instructive. As we might expect, the twenty-three traceable cases whose legal residence in 1148 was given as the occupied area of North China—largely, no doubt, refugees or sons of refugees from the Jurchen invasion— were nearly 70 per cent officially-connected. In 1256 there was only one such case, a new man from a place near the Sung border. For the territories under Sung control, the regions having high proportions of new men seem to share certain characteristics which are rather different from the unifying characteristics we saw in regions with many degrees per capita. The several regions vary greatly in the backgrounds of their graduates, but on the whole a high proportion of new men seems as likely to appear in a thinly populated region as in one more densely populated and economically developed. There does, however, seem to be a correlation between population *change* and the proportion of new men. In general, a long-range population rise tends to accompany a higher proportion of new men, while a long period of population stability or fall seems often to accompany a larger proportion of officially-connected graduates. . . .

To oversimplify the picture somewhat, under the circumstances of free interregional competition a given circuit tended to fall into one or another of the following patterns of associated characteristics:

POPULATION	DENSE, RISING	SPARSE, RISING	DENSE, NOT RISING	SPARSE, NOT RISING
Graduates per capita	Many	Few	Many	Few
Ratio of new men	High	High	Low	Low
Number of new men	Many	Rather few	Rather many	Few

The coincidence of rising populations and high proportions of new men may be explainable as the result of greater social mobility among new settlers, who were able in their new homes to raise both their economic and their social status. In this connection it is interesting to note that three southeastern circuits with many new men in one year or both—Che-tung, Fu-chien, and Chiang-nan Tung—show in 1256 an unusually high number of graduates whose actual homes are elsewhere than their official residences. (Data on this are not available for 1148.) These may well be either immigrants or descendants of immigrants. This possibility in itself would have interesting implications for Sung society; it is linked with another factor that gives it still greater interest. For we find that in the Sung dynasty there were important areas that fell into the pattern of dense and rising population and higher proportions of new men. These areas included two of the most populous and urbanized circuits—Che-tung and Fu-chien. These two together furnished over a third of the new men from all of China in both 1148 and 1256. Even in the eleventh century we saw that they contributed a high proportion of the doctors of letters.

Do we have here, in the fact that southeastern urbanization was in its *active* phase, the controlling factor in the social mobility of the Sung civil service? Before a final answer can be given, it will be necessary to look into additional factors not here considered which may also have influenced the accessibility of the examinations to different social groups. The relative availability of educational facilities, the subject matter prescribed, and the examiners' methods all contributed to the result. The currents of economic development were themselves complex. But we can scarcely doubt that the degree of free opportunity present in the Sung examinations owed much to a combination of circumstances peculiar to the period—the continued growth of population in the urbanized and commercial southeastern coastal regions and a freedom of competition that allowed this region to dominate the examinations as a whole.

From what social groups did these new men come? If commercial development and city growth were related to the influx of new blood into the bureaucracy through the examinations, to what extent were the merchants or their families represented? Evidence on this point is not yet sufficient for a satisfactory answer; it seems at least quite possible that the share of the merchants among the new men was considerable. Social bars against them were weakening, and we know that a number held government positions. Yet, if they contributed any significant number to the civil service, there is as yet little evidence that they retained their group identity or exercised any strong influence on government policies. In many ways the sources of the new men among Sung graduates, and their political role, remain an enigma.

4. THE ERA OF REGIONAL QUOTAS

The extinction of the Sung dynasty in 1279 marked, in one sense, the end of an era in the Chinese examination system. The regime of relatively unrestricted competition among candidates, with the empire as a single arena, gave way to systems of regional quotas. Apart from the rivalry for high placement, the individual candidate was now really pitted only against others of his region. The distribution of opportunity among regions was now subject to political decision. The southeastern coast lost its preferential position, and new factors came to affect the rise of new men. . . . When the Mongol rulers decided in 1315 to revive the examinations, then long suspended, they adapted the quota principle to purposes of their own. Obliged to use Chinese administrative skills in running their new empire, yet distrusting Chinese loyalty, they balanced carefully the several racial elements that comprised their bureaucracy. They curtailed the number of examination degrees to a yearly average of a little over twenty-one, which contrasted sharply with the Sung yearly average of around two hundred. The examinations now clearly played a more limited role in the recruitment of the bureaucracy. The degrees were divided equally among the four recognized racial groups: Mongols, foreign collaborators of the Mongols (*Se-mu jen*), North Chinese (*Han-jen*), and South Chinese (*Nan-jen*). In terms of population, and no doubt of potential candidates, this division greatly favored the Mongols and their foreign collaborators, the most trusted groups, and, among the Chinese, it favored those of the North over those of the South. . . .

The Ming house, which expelled the Mongols and restored China's independ-ence in 1368, tended to pursue a policy of modifying Mongol practices without reverting entirely to previous Chinese traditions. . . . The Ming at first discarded the Mongol system of regional quotas, but the men of the Southeast soon began once more to win the lion's share of the degrees, and in 1425 fixed proportions were allocated to the North and to the South. The division was later made threefold, allowing for a Middle Quota Region in addition to the Northern and Southern. The new Middle Region included a small but populous area in the East, roughly equivalent to the part of modern Anhwei north of the Yangtze, and a large area in the Southwest, where Szechwan and Yunnan had become under the Mongols more closely identified with the North than with the South. The *chü-jen*, or "master's," degrees, qualifying a candidate to compete in the doctoral examinations, increased in importance. Under the Ming, as under the Mongols, each province was allowed a fixed number of these.

The threefold division of doctoral quotas remained, with temporary interruptions, for the rest of the dynasty. Under the Ch'ing dynasty of the Manchus, the division was further elaborated by the assignment of numerical doctoral quotas for each province, in lieu of the regional percentages, and by the addition of quotas for Chinese, Mongol, and Manchu bannermen who chose the examinations as a path of advancement. It is not altogether clear how far the Ming and Ch'ing quotas reflected the local distribution of potential candidates. In terms of the total regional populations, the quotas assigned seem for the most part rather fair. The 55 per cent assigned to the Southern Quota Region and the 10 per cent assigned to the Middle in 1426 may well have been close to their respective shares of the population at that time, although the northward migration perceptible in the Mongol and Ming periods may have left the South with a more favorable ratio of quota to population during the later Ming. The provincial quotas for master's degrees in the Ming and for doctor's in the Ch'ing period (varying slightly from year to year) in general appear to recognize the changed population pattern; the numbers assigned to the individual provinces during the nineteenth century, however, tend to favor the more thinly settled at the expense of the more populous.

But representation in terms of population was only one aspect of regional representation. We must remember that the distribution of potential candidates might be quite unequal in different regions; in terms of the quality of their preparation, it might be still more unequal. Where opportunities for education varied locally, regional quotas that ignored this variation necessarily created differences in the intensity of competition. These differences would favor the man in the region which had fewer and inferior candidates (in terms of the standards then accepted). As we have seen, the evidence of the Sung examination lists tends to confirm the supposition that the more numerous and better qualified candidates came from regions of denser population. In these regions, if quotas were equalized on a per capita basis, the competition would be keenest. Which candidates would win out? Very possibly those with official connections and the associated advantages of education, family tradition, and experience. In the twelfth and thirteenth centuries, at least, the men without official connections tended to appear more frequently among the lower grade-brackets of the examination lists, and this situation may well have persisted. Thus in more densely populated regions the quota restriction, other things being equal, would tend to eliminate larger numbers of new men. Other regional conditions affecting social mobility might modify this effect or exaggerate it.

For the Mongol and Ming periods there seems to be as yet no quantitative evidence to test the outcome. For the Ch'ing period, however, we are more fortunate. For some years scholars at the University of Washington have gathered from many sources an impressive body of evidence on nineteenth-century Chinese institutions. . . . This evidence throws interesting light on certain aspects of the problem of social mobility in the later Ch'ing period. In the nineteenth century, as in the twelfth and thirteenth, the proportions of new men in the several areas show much evidence of constancy within limited periods, but there are noticeable contrasts between the pre-quota periods (before 1279) and the nineteenth century. In the latter, there is a rather constant tendency toward higher ratios of new men among the doctoral graduates in the provinces of lesser population density, notably Kweichow, Shensi, and Kansu. There is also, it is true, some tendency toward a similar higher ratio of new men in provinces that show more rapid population growth during the century. But while such growing and relatively urbanized provinces as Kwangtung and Hupeh show such a combination of social mobility and growth, they are also among those with more limited per capita representation among the graduates, so that they do not affect the national averages as much as they otherwise might. It is tempting to find here an example in which the quota system worked to reduce social mobility in the examinations as a whole. But since the doctoral figures are based on a study still in progress, such inferences must be tempered with caution.

The holders of lower degrees and equivalent ranks in the Ch'ing offer in some ways a better comparison with the Sung doctoral degrees, although factors other than the regular examinations affect the picture. The proportion of new men as a whole is significantly greater among lower-degree holders than among the doctoral-degree holders of the same period; there are also other differences. Dr. Chang [Chung-li] notes several factors that throw light on the regional pattern. The relative administrative importance of an area plays a large role. It would appear that the generous quotas accorded the border provinces were meant to encourage the supply of trained men to help in the informal chores of local administration in those underpopulated areas. Some of the highest proportions of new men are found in Ch'ing provinces whose people had received expanded graduate quotas after 1850, either because they had played a more active part in fighting the Taiping and other rebels or because they had contributed generously to the depleted state treasury. In this category may fall the province of Hunan, with its population of medium density, as well as the border provinces of Yunnan and Kweichow. Commercial wealth also may have accounted for the high proportions of new men from such populous provinces as Anhwei and Kwangtung. Increasingly generous examination quotas were now specially reserved for the merchants as a group. In addition, degrees and ranks were now opened to purchase on a far greater scale than before, and provinces such as Anhwei and Kwangtung were high among the beneficiaries of this practice. Merchants may well have been among the leading purchasers.

Through one channel or another, it appears from this evidence that the emergency caused by the rebellions opened an opportunity to previously untapped sources of new men and, in doing so, underlined the fact that these men might otherwise have had no opportunity for entrance into the civil service. While the examinations clearly remained a vital tool of state policy, the emphasis and purposes of the system had changed since the thirteenth century in significant respects. Perhaps the expansion of the educated group over the intervening centuries made it less vital to seek out qualified men, regardless of their region, solely on the basis of their qualifications. The merit principle could now be tempered by political considerations. At the same time, as we have seen, other ways of advancement assumed greater importance for the new men as alternative entrances into the bureaucracy.

The shifting balance of regional importance may also have contributed to the changing examination policies. It would seem that in a sense the pendulum had returned, in the course of twelve centuries, to its original position. The movement away from regional discrimination had begun in the T'ang, when the growing importance of the South enabled it to serve as a useful political counterweight to the hitherto dominant northern groups. The examinations served the southerners well, and seemingly furthered the growth of their own political and intellectual leadership even before the North was lost by conquest. After the fall of the Sung, however, the North reasserted its political role, and at the same time the southward flow of population was reversed. A century and a half of separation and divergent experience no doubt strengthened regional differences and sharpened regional rivalries, present even in earlier times. But since the men of the South were not easily surpassed in the literary skills, the quota was a convenient weapon for a Northern reassertion of political influence.

Thus, in the single narrow aspect of the examination system that has been the focus of this paper, we find that in the course of centuries the dominant trend of Chinese opinion has continued for the most part to recognize the need for equal opportunity in the examinations. In defining the desirable form of "equal opportunity," however, political conditions of different periods have led to shifting formulations, which have stressed variously equality for the individual, the racial group, or the region.

THE ATTEMPT TO MEASURE TALENT

Qualification for Office: Expertise or Character?

HEINZ FRIESE

When the Ming dynasty lifted the ban which had excluded the sons of merchants and artisans from the examinations, the chances for recruiting able commoners into the civil service broadened. Yet the road by which such newcomers might enter officialdom became, if anything, narrower during the Ming. Only a classical education attested by examination could transform the sons of craftsmen into gentlemen fit to rule the realm.

Heinz Friese, a German sinologist from Hamburg, shows here that the status of craftsmen who served the government in their capacity as higher artisans remained controversial. Were they to be given official status if their services, however technical, were of undoubted benefit to the state? His examination of Ming data leads Professor Friese to raise important questions about the nature and range of excellency which the Chinese state sought in its "men of talent."

FROM the Cheng-te period [1506–22] on, we find scattered references in the sources concerning craftsmen who rose into officialdom on the basis of outstanding achievement. We find reported by name, for instance, the case of a carpenter, Hsü Kao who rose to be president of the Ministry of Works during the Chia-ching period [1522–66]. He is supposed to have owed this high ascent to the favor of the Emperor Shih-tsung [i.e. Chia-ching]. Once, in 1540, when he was slighted in a promotion, the Emperor personally took matters in hand and punished the responsible official in the Ministry of Personnel by curtailment of salary. By 1558, Hsü Kao is listed as secretary (rank 3a) of the Ministry of Works. One of his sons had already previously been nominated deputy inspector of the office in charge of fine work in gold, silver, ivory, and jade (rank 9b) at his father's request and on the basis of the yin-privilege. In that capacity, he was responsible for supervising construction work on the spot. Since crafts were hereditary in families, he, like his father, had probably been trained as a carpenter and was thus well suited to this office. It was Hsü Kao's constant concern to launch all of his sons in official careers. In subsequent years, he made three petitions in this connection. For his second son, he requested the office of a company commander in the imperial body guard, and for the third son he wanted the office of a supervisor in the directorate of ceremonial (rank 9b). The Ministry of War considered this improper, but the emperor, pointing to Hsü Kao's exceptional merits, conferred on the third son the office of a commander of the guard. A report by Hsü Chie makes clear that Hsü Kao must indeed have been indispensable to the Emperor Shih-tsung. The author of the report remarked that the emperor would undoubtedly be in trouble in respect to architectural projects if he had

From Heinz Friese, "Zum Aufstieg von Handwerkern ins Beamtentum während der Ming-Zeit," *Oriens Extremus*, VI (1959), pp. 161–172. Reprinted by permission. [Editor's translation. In translating titles of officials and offices, I have as far as possible adopted the terminology of Professor Charles O. Hucker. A translated document which a ppeared in an appendix has been omitted.]

to make do without Hsü Kao's service for even a day. He furthermore reported that the constant rewards and proofs of imperial favor led to envy and calumny on the part of the regular officialdom and that for this reason Hsü Kao had to live in continual fear. He exerted all his powers to "shut up the crowd." In this spirit, the author of the report asked that for the sake of Hsü's safety no more awards be bestowed. Indeed, Hsü fell at the very moment when Emperor Mu-tsung ascended the throne (1566). Immediately, voices were raised urging that he be deprived of his offices. He, an artisan, it was said, had dared to ride in a palanquin carried by eight runners! This indicates clearly that despite the high office he held, Hsü was not recognized by Confucian officialdom and continued to be, in their eyes, an upstart. What they resented particularly was that Hsü had helped many hundreds of artisans who worked under him to gain positions in officialdom. Eventually he was tried for embezzlement of state funds and hounded from office. In the light of the foregoing, it may be doubted that this accusation had any substance, especially since in another source Hsü had been praised for his frugality and modesty. He was not included in the collections of biographies, a really remarkable omission for one who held such high office.

Another artisan whom we know by name was one Lu Hsiang, a stonemason from Wu-hsi in South Chihli. He rose from foreman to senior vice minister in the Ministry of Works, after having been active for many years in the construction bureau and having shown exceptional skill in supervising construction activities. As an example of his artistic skill, the story is told of a square stone on which he once engraved a pond in which fishes, dragons and algae could be seen. This stone, intended as a present for a superior official, is supposed to have expressed his consummate art. He was praised for decorum and courtesy. He also seems to have been popular because on one occasion when his mother fell ill, his superior officials immediately acted on his behalf and prevailed upon the salary office to send the mother a daily ration of wine, food, and money. It is said that officialdom did not resent him as it did others who had attained official rank by irregular means. His son was later also raised to official rank. The very emphasis on the friendly attitude of officialdom toward this man probably indicates that it was the exception, not the rule.

The case of the carpenter K'uai Hsiang, likewise from South Chihli and subsequently junior vice minister in the Ministry of Works, is similar. In the year 1457 he and Lu Hsiang together are recorded as holding that post. Both were ordered to supervise public construction projects. At this time, K'uai already received the salary of an official of the second rank, a sign that he enjoyed high favor. He also was decorous and considerate toward other officials and, in spite of his high office, remained frugal and modest. It was he who built the palaces in Peking for the Yung-lo Emperor. He is said to have remained active and in office until the age of eighty-four. In the end, it is even reported, he received the salary of an official of the first rank. Two of his sons were also raised to official rank on the basis of the *yin*-privilege.

Although artisans frequently attained high honors in this fashion, it is difficult to locate or compile their biographies. This alone indicates how strongly the "gentry" opposed the entry into its ranks of people who lacked the qualification based on state examinations. Such people were simply ignored. In the case of Lu Hsiang and K'uai Hsiang there were probably ethical motives which caused the historians to record the lives of these men. We may draw the following conclusion: According to the prevailing opinion of Confucian officialdom, a man of humble origin who had risen to high office should always preserve a respectful distance toward his colleagues in officialdom, mindful of his humble past. He was supposed to retain always his simple and modest way of life, as did K'uai Hsiang, who had never mounted an official palanquin. Nor should such a man dare request an official position for his son, as did Ts'ai Hsin, junior vice minister of the Ministry of Works and a former artisan. He had requested that his son be charged in his place with the supervision of construction works. This was permitted. But when shortly thereafter he requested that his son be made an official, the Emperor refused indignantly, and the Ministry of Works requested that his salary be held up. What seems to have determined the attitudes of regular officialdom in all these cases was not so much the social background of the craftsmen who had risen to high posts, but their lack of the regular educational qualifications.

Although the biographical material for cases like these is very sparse, we can gain an approximate idea of the extent of such ascents of craftsmen into officialdom. Especially during the Cheng-te reign (1506–22) which was dominated by the eunuch Liu Chin, such appointments to office seem to have been frequent. Strangely, there are few relevant sources dating from this period. Only in the Chia-ching period did people begin, retrospectively, to point to this state of affairs, and to try to curb or undo what had been done. In his speech from the throne Emperor Shih-tsung remarked in 1522 that since the first year of Cheng-te (1506), "people of different kinds" had moved into lower and higher officialdom. He especially mentioned monks and artisans. The ministries were ordered to review their personnel with this in mind and to dismiss such officials. A few years later, Grand Secretary Yang I-ch'ing advised in a memorandum that the eunuch offices should be ordered not to nominate any other artisans and soldiers for appointment in the civil service. It was no longer a matter of dismissals, but simply of restrictions of future appointments. Indeed, a considerable number of such appointments must have been involved; in one record, thousands are mentioned. It almost

seems as if it had been decided to accept a *fait accompli* when, shortly thereafter, an order was issued not to place into civil offices those military artisans who had attained official rank, and not to place into the imperial guard any of the civilian artisans.

Nor was the attitude of the Emperor consistent. This can be seen from the following examples: in 1522, the director of the directorate of imperial utensils requested the promotion of fifty-two weavers. The responsible officials in the Ministry of Works objected and said: "In return for their skill, the state supports the craftsmen. They are only meant to weave. How dare one raise such unjustified hopes in their minds and show them favors to such an extent! The evil of such requests should be stopped by imperial order. If one truly wants to reward their merits, it would be sufficient to present them with gold and brocade." The Emperor evaded a decision and chose the golden mean, as he often did. He ordered that twenty-five weavers be appointed inspectors in the leather processing office; the other twenty-seven had to be content with two ounces of silver and some rolls of silk each. A similar incident occurred in the following year, when the director of the directorate of palace attendants upon conclusion of construction work on some palaces requested that one hundred and sixty artisans be appointed to the rank of bursars (7b) and secretaries (8b) in Shun-t'ien fu [the metropolitan prefecture]. The responsible official in the Ministry of Personnel refused firmly, but the Emperor did not listen to him. The last example illustrates that in several cases the eunuchs even went so far as to appoint their favored artisans directly into administrative offices.

It is hard to say exactly when these appointments began; the earliest records date already from the beginning of the T'ien-shun period. In the year 1457, for instance, nine artisans and cooks from the circuits of Ta Hsing and Wan P'ing were appointed company commanders in the imperial guard. Several years later, six others were promoted to inspectors in the office in charge of fine work in gold, silver, ivory, and jade. In 1499, thirty-nine artisans were appointed to the same position; twenty-three others obtained the office of inspectors of the leather processing office, while another sixteen craftsmen of the embroidery office who had already been decorated with official's hats and girdles, were given the office of deputy inspector. On the occasion of these appointments it was added that all of them should continue their former occupations. This probably meant that all these artisans, even when they obtained low official rank and an official's salary, had to remain at their old places of work—in a workshop or on a construction site—of course, in leading positions. Later, on the other hand, the path to other agencies seems to have opened for them. The first step, however, always was a technical office in the Ministry of Works or in one of the eunuch offices.[1] The appointment to officialdom was usually preceded by the award of an official's hat and girdle which freed them from physical labor.

It must have been undoubtedly beneficial for the development of technology that experts were put in leading positions. Perhaps it had even proved necessary to give to the many technicians who guarded so large a part of China's cultural treasures the necessary prestige that would enable them to work freely. One need but imagine that the builders of the great palaces and temples, whose construction required the highest technical competency, were recruited according to a forced draft system which conferred on its draftees the status, roughly, of slave-labor! If we think of all the technical branches, shipbuilding or dam building—technical direction and planning was always in the hands of artisans, not of officials. The artisans designed the blueprints and personally supervised the work. Therefore one may consider it

[1] What Professor Hucker calls "Service Agencies of the Imperial Household," largely staffed by eunuchs. [Editor's note]

meritorious that the eunuch officials tried to gain for these technical experts a social position consistent with their importance. This is true even if the motives which impelled the eunuchs were other than those which they officially admitted. They were only concerned with having personal adherents in officialdom who would advance their own interests. Given this motive, it was fortunate that the eunuchs were far less conservative than regular officialdom and lacked the latter's status consciousness.

All these irregular promotions were carried out on the pretext that the persons concerned had special achievements to their credit. Officially, the merit principle was recognized in the case of soldiers, but not for civilians, although the eunuchs, semi-officially, seem to have applied it to the latter also, against heavy opposition from regular officialdom. Ch'iu Chün [a high official] pointed out that such a practice could only undermine the morale of the soldiers who would no longer be ready to risk their lives in war for rewards to which craftsmen had access as a matter of course. Furthermore, he pointed out that artisans who had been so distinguished would only be the butt of general joking so that even for them it did not amount to a distinction; everybody knew that no true merit was involved. It was a completely impossible situation, Ch'iu Chün finally remarked, if offices of such persons were made hereditary. The president of the Ministry of War, Wang Shu, memorialized as follows:

In the time of Hung-wu and Yung-lo [founder and third emperor of the Ming, respectively] the number of officials was restricted. There were no positions at the imperial court for soldiers of fortune. Therefore only the wise and capable were in office and those who lived on official salaries were few. In recent times, however, more and more persons daily are promoted without merit and advance despite incompetence. Artisans and artists, run-away homeless fellows, people who work in magical arts and others manage to gain rewarding official positions through crooked paths. Men in official dress throng the markets in the morning. This is truly a senseless waste of the fund for official salaries and, in addition, it does damage to the gifted. For in this way one cannot provide incentives for the wise and able, nor promote men of merit. From now on, civil offices should be bestowed only on persons who have the qualifications of *chin-shih,* or *chien-sheng* or who are lesser functionaries. Military offices must be filled only with personnel who have gained merit in the military field. Those [above mentioned] persons who have already been placed in irregular civil offices should all be registered by name and then sent home until such time as vacancies occur. Then they may be used, provided the Ministry of Personnel has examined their qualifications. The physicians, soothsayers and artisans who have risen to official rank must be ordered to return to their original occupations. They should simply be given a *tan* of rice [in place of official salaries]. Whatever amounts they have received beyond this sum, should be retained and all their servants should be dismissed. . . .

Only one exception was admitted. Those officials who had been promoted prior to the eleventh year of Ch'eng-hua (1475) might stay in office. It was proposed:

. . . Officials who have originally been musicians and dancers may only be employed in the imperial office of ceremonial; former astrologers only in the office of astrology; former physicians only in the imperial medical office; and former artisans only in the planning office and construction office of the Ministry of Works.

This was combined with the urgent request to exclude such officials from all other offices—from the six ministries and from the provincial administration offices. Since this matter was stressed so emphatically, it may be assumed that such irregularly promoted officials had indeed penetrated into administrative offices. On the other hand, it becomes clear that this was true not only of former artisans, but also of other professions.

As we have already indicated, the irregular promotions were chiefly due to the

initiative of eunuch officials. On the basis of their position in the palace, the eunuchs could at any time make out patents of nomination signed by the emperor—whether his signature was faked or not need not detain us here—thus bypassing the Ministry of Personnel. This practice, known as the *ch'uan-feng,* had become a much criticized abuse. In this connection, the following description is revealing:

Recently (1483) commoners, money slaves, merchants, craftsmen, deposed officials and sons of the gentry everywhere approach the eunuchs through all sorts of intrigues and make them costly presents. Immediately they are rewarded with official posts, as for instance the position of deputy director of the directorate of ceremonial (rank 3b), secretaries of provincial administration offices (rank 6b), and supervisory officials in the Chancellery of State. People who are promoted on the basis of patents made out by eunuchs are called "*ch'uan-feng.*"
. . . presently, the officials in the capital number 1200. The ch'uan-feng officials number up to 800.

Another source confirms these figures. It furthermore speaks of two hundred and eighty military *ch'uan-feng,* and adds that a great number of them are relatives of eunuchs. The Censor Chang Chi even spoke of "butchers of dogs and sellers of pictures" who now suddenly assume the airs of great lords. "People who have no knowledge whatever are arbitrarily entrusted with civil office; and people who have never shot an arrow are given military office on some pretext," he complains.

The patrons of such nominations were to be found not only among the eunuchs. In this connection, there is a record of a man by the name of Li Tzu-sheng who held various high offices in the Ch'eng-hua period (1464–88). Originally, he had been a scribe. Through his knowledge of Taoist magic, he came in touch with eunuchs. It was probably at their suggestion that he was given office. He stood high in the favor of the Emperor, over whom he had great influence because of his magic arts.

Due to his influence, it is said, hundreds of persons without examination degrees were appointed to officialdom at once, especially Buddhist and Taoist monks. . . .

All these officials who lacked examination degrees were called *Tsa-liu* in Chinese terminology. This category included also students of the imperial academy who acquired office by purchase, or persons who had been decorated with official rank for having donated grain to the state in times of economic distress. The most discussed problem, however, was that of the . . . scribes. From T'ang times on, the appointment of able scribes to official posts seems to have become something of a customary right. Liang Fang-chung explains that whereas in T'ang and Sung times the gentry considered such an official career shameful, during Mongol times the distinction between regular officials and those who had originally been scribes had become almost blurred; indeed, the latter came to be in the majority and were better off; he maintains that there existed for a time a veritable "regime of scribes." The first Ming emperors followed this practice. Even among the presidents of ministries one could encounter former scribes, for instance, the presidents of the Ministry of War, Hsü Hsi and Wang Chi. Many others became censors and the number of those who held lower positions was immeasurably large. All of them are supposed to have been recommended by their superiors according to the *pao-chien* [recommendation] system and are said, in the main, to have given an excellent account of themselves. It was regretted that after the Ch'eng-hua period, when the system of recommendation decayed, the scribes lacked this possibility for promotion. It was regretted particularly because the chance to rise to gentry rank had served as an incentive for them to cultivate the literary arts and to pursue the Confucian *chün-tzu* ideal. Furthermore, because of the decay of the system, the state lost many people with great administrative ability. In other words, it was not shameful for a scribe to be recommended for official appointment. Such persons were never mentioned in one breath with artisans, monks, and merchants although under official terminology they fell into the same category. After all, they entered officialdom by a regular path, that of recommendation. The system of recommendation had been used to supplement the rigid and impersonal procedure of the examination system, in that it considered factors of personality and guaranteed the moral integrity of officials in the process of recruitment. Its abolition introduced a regrettable rigidity into the official career. The recommendation system had made it possible to bring able and technically qualified personnel into high officialdom, by-passing if necessary the strict rules of examination and official advancement. This possibility was virtually closed after the Ch'eng-hua period. Consequently, official careers now came to follow one rigid pattern with hardly any deviations. Hu Shih-ning expressed it as follows: "The way by which officials are chosen has become narrow. Therefore it is no wonder that it is so difficult to find qualified personnel." Whereas previously there existed great leeway in the use of special talents and while officials could be used according to their individual talents and abilities, now everyone more or less had to follow the same pattern. Hu said: "The path of promotion for all these many officials depends exclusively on the position from which they happen to start. . . . Nobody takes into account the results of their practical experience during a lifetime in office. If a *chin-shih,* when first appointed, gets a good post, he will have his routine promotions and will end up in an influential position. But if he should ever be placed in some kind of marginal post, he will stay all his life in a subordinate position, no matter what his talents." Thus, the efforts of all young aspirants for office are directed to securing a good starting position, in some way or other. The offices in the capital are the most favored. If, however, a post in Nanking[2] becomes vacant, they all try to avoid being appointed. Even more unpopular are censorial appointments, because in such positions one quickly earns the anger of superiors and is then dismissed. All are out for personal advantage alone; no one is willing to take any risks. What should one expect from such servants of the state in times of emergency, Hu asks himself.

It is against this background that the many irregular appointments of craftsmen, monks, and merchants were made. When the path of recommendation closed, another, that of *ch'uan-feng*, began to open. But there is an essential difference between the two. In the case of recommendation, what matters are not so much merit and achievement, but moral qualities as defined by Confucian ethics. In the case of irregular appointments, only merit and achievement play a role, that is, strictly practical criteria. It is striking that an official is judged much less by his actions and the outwardly visible effect of these actions than by whether or not he approximates, in personal and moral conduct, the qualities of character of the Confucian ideal

[2] In Nanking, capital of the founder of the Ming dynasty, a full complement of government offices was maintained although the absence of the court made it, politically speaking, a backwater. [Editor's note]

type. Virtue, which resides in him and represents a spontaneously acting, regulating force, is assigned more weight than sheer ability. Ability can only be proven in practical life. This type of personality rating gave the Confucian-educated official very little incentive to emerge from his passive attitude and to direct his intellectual faculties to practical pursuits. May one not see in this attitude one of the reasons why intellectual activity and technical interest seemed forever incompatible? In all the discussions about irregular appointments, the key question really was whether achievement in any field—except the military—without moral qualification entitled a man to a post in officialdom. The answer clearly was no. The fact that so many persons who lacked the requisite training nevertheless managed to enter the official class may indicate that the rigidity of the official hierarchy had to be counterbalanced in some form or other. The administration undoubtedly needed a certain number of technical experts. The system of recommendation had managed to satisfy this need up to a certain point while keeping access under control. But from the middle of the Ming on, certain factors injected themselves into the process which were outside the control of officialdom and led to its disintegration. . . .

Sponsorship and the Selection of Talent

E. A. KRACKE, JR.

The examination method widened the chances for able commoners to enter officialdom, but it did not necessarily assure the recruitment of "men of talent." From the Confucian point of view, the examination method suffered, almost as much as it benefited, from the impersonality and objectivity of its procedures. Personal judgment and appraisal alone, it was thought, could guarantee the choice of men of real worth.

In this selection, Professor Kracke discusses the attempts of Sung statesmen to work out an alternative procedure for the selection and promotion of worthy officials. Not concerned with quantitative data nor with the social background of civil servants, Professor Kracke's study of sponsorship focusses on a new aspect of the "career open to talent."

ADMINISTRATIVE RESPONSIBILITY
IN THE CONFUCIAN STATE

As ancient Greece and mediaeval England created many of the most vital traditions of representative government, so Confucian China evolved much that has entered the common heritage of personnel administration in the modern state. China early developed techniques to promote the recruitment and advancement of government employees on the basis of ability, and to minimize the role of political patronage. It pioneered also in applying techniques to maintain honesty, discipline, and initiative —in other words, administrative responsibility—among government personnel. This . . . is a study of such techniques when they first attained substantially their modern form [in the early Sung period, 960–1067 A.D.]; . . . the segment selected . . . is the policy of promotion through controlled sponsorship (*pao jen*). . . . In

its simplest essentials, this technique consisted in granting special promotions within the service on the recommendation of a superior officer, who thereafter was legally answerable for the quality and the acts of his protégé. Systematized and elaborated, the technique was found suitable for use on a large scale to meet widely varied situations and became a regular practice in Chinese personnel administration. . . .

Just as examinations and merit rating procedures grew slowly from the older Confucian doctrine, sponsorship also had its roots in the past. The two elements which were combined in sponsorship— recommendation for public office and the recommender's responsibility for the character of his protégé—go far back in Chinese history. . . . From the earliest clearly historical times, recommendation was not merely sanctioned as an open practice; the recommendation of worthy and able men

Reprinted by permission of the publishers from E. A. Kracke, Jr., *Civil Service in Early Sung China, 960–1067*, pp. 1–2, 6–7, 54, 58, 84–86, 102, 104, 115–119, 126, 130–132, 136, 138–141, 144, 146, 152, 155, 168–169, 186–187, 194–198. Cambridge, Mass.: Harvard University Press. Copyright, 1953, by Harvard-Yenching Institute.

became at least a moral obligation, possibly reinforced by penalties for its neglect. By the early second century B.C., if not earlier, recommendation had assumed institutional form. . . .

The time at which a legal responsibility became associated with recommendation is less easily determined. The open and formal nature of the act of recommendation in itself served to place the credit or blame for a recommendation on the recommender. This responsibility may have been transformed, by the Han dynasty, into a legal guaranty. . . .

THE CIVIL SERVICE: ITS RECRUITMENT AND ADVANCEMENT

[Under] the early Sung rulers . . . the numbers recruited into the civil service were greatly expanded by methods which stressed particularly the merit principle. . . . New methods of promotion were devised. . . . Methods of civil service recruitment . . . fell into three major categories: recruitment through examination, through transfer from other services, and through protection [i.e. the *yin* privilege]. . . . It is very difficult to determine the exact relative importance of the three major methods. The examination far surpassed all others in prestige. Each of the three seems to have accounted for the recruitment of a significant proportion of the total number of [active] officials, but by the end of the century under consideration the number of offices filled by holders of examination degrees may have considerably exceeded the combined total filled by other methods. . . .

The practices by which a civil servant was assigned to his rank and function, and advanced from one step of the structure to another . . . were in considerable degree specified by rules. . . . [The rules] were planned to ensure that ability might rise rapidly to high position, without disregarding the need for experience.

As these objectives were to some extent conflicting, so were the methods which embodied them. Advancement depended on a number of factors. From the first we find that the more important controlling factors included regular positional sequence, and set terms of office, modified in application by preferential treatment based on the way in which the service had been entered, and by the use of merit ratings, examinations for promotion, and sponsorship. . . .

The relative emphasis to be placed on the different factors was the subject of continuous controversy. This reflected a more fundamental difference of opinion: the contest between those who advocated a government of laws, on the one hand, and on the other those who held that good government was to be achieved only through officials of high character, who could not be found by any rule. The conflict was clearly stated by Su Shih [Sung statesman and poet]. He says: "It will surely be argued that if a distinction is made on the basis of relative ability, without a wholly fixed law, then private likes and dislikes have an opening. I do not consider this to be so. The thing with law is to preserve its basic principles; its additions, subtractions, and evolution will certainly be entrusted to men. . . . If someone insists that one must trust laws, not men; that one certainly cannot place confidence in the men of the world, and needs a fixed rule; I still am not convinced that such a course cannot result in depravity."

. . . As time passes, however, there appears a closer integration of the various factors into a single complex but less variable pattern. Rapidity of advancement comes to depend not on any single factor, but on a combination of all factors. . . .

With the tendency toward systematization, the official of average abilities seems to have acquired a better chance of advancement, while the chances of rapid rise through good fortune or superior ability seem to have diminished correspondingly. Sponsorship, important from the beginning, played a role of ever growing importance as a normal channel of promotion. . . .

SCOPE AND OBJECTIVES
OF SPONSORSHIP

. . . Its place was in some ways intermediate; it was less selective and affected larger numbers than did the [advancement] examinations, but it was more selective than promotion through sequence and tenure, [or] merit rating. . . .

The most obvious objective of those who promoted sponsorship . . . was simply to find the man best qualified for a post or rank which, whether high or low, was critically important, and to speed the rise of the able man to the place where he was most needed. . . .

The documents which embody early Sung policy on sponsorship describe with great care the qualities which a candidate should have. . . .

It is not surprising that personal character, which occupied such an important place in Confucian political theory, received stress in sponsorship. [Sponsorship] seemed, of all Sung promotion methods, the best adapted to favor the man of worth, the *hsien-jen*. Those who complained of the character of officials in their day often turned to sponsorship as the most promising tool of reform. Though they often perceived its shortcomings in practice, they looked for remedies through its improvement rather than the substitution of other methods.

When they translated the general stress on worth into more specific terms, the traits most often called for were rather more concrete and practical than we might have expected after reading the eulogies on the worthies of old with which measures were often prefaced. Vigor, for instance, stood near the top of the list. Most often it was sought in the forms of effort, achievement, and industry. Somewhat less often— and especially for more important positions —there was emphasis on firmness and freedom from timidity.

Discipline was mentioned even more often than vigor. Most often it appeared as freedom from the misuse of authority, presumption, or impropriety. It also took the positive form of reliability, or understanding of the proper code of a public servant.

Caution is among traits sought for more important posts. . . .

But far greater than the concern with all these traits was that shown by the innumerable stipulations that the candidate show a record free from corruption and penal offense. These last considerations were of course vital to the functioning of the government. They were in addition criteria which could be applied far more objectively than some of the others mentioned.

In describing the kind of man eligible for recommendation, the proclamations showed the concern of their authors with administrative ability, training acquired through study or practice, and experience as indicated by positions previously held and length of service. . . .

The training specified was most often general, with the customary emphasis on classics, literature, and history. . . .

It was understood that a part of the civil servant's training could be acquired only through actual experience with administrative problems. It was not desirable to recommend a man who had but recently entered the service because he "might not yet be versed in the requirements of an official position.". . .

The requirements of experience, which we have just seen, ruled out as sponsorship candidate the untried newcomer in the service. In contrast with these, a different set of requirements sought to rule out also the man whose friendships or abilities had already ensured him notice. At least three considerations focussed the attention of sponsorship on the man without influential connections and in a relatively obscure position. First, much of the unique value of recommendation lay in its potential effectiveness in discovering able men who might otherwise be overlooked. Second, personal considerations, whether through connection of the sponsored with the sponsor or with any other party, might impede objective recommendation on the basis of merit. Third, there was constant awareness of the lurking danger that a faction in contemporary ascendancy might achieve a perpetual power monopoly, using recommendation as a tool. . . .

Although sponsorship was primarily a device to recruit men for more important positions in the civil service, . . . this was not its sole concern. It is evident that the system was designed also to encourage better performance in the service as a whole. The aim was to be reached through affording fairer treatment to the individual who might otherwise be slighted unjustly. It offered greater hope of a successful career to the man who, while able and conscientious as an administrator, lacked the scholarly talents needed to take and pass the special examinations for promotion. It gave the supervisory official a means of rewarding good performance more concretely than through merit ratings which . . . were not in practice too effective.

THE PROCEDURES AND POLICIES OF SPONSORSHIP

In order to find men of the kind and quality desired for positions so many and so varied, it was obviously necessary to construct an elaborate apparatus to administer the sponsorship process. In the adaptation to institutional use, the simple act of recommendation was transformed into a complex series of procedures. Rules governed each step, from the decision to employ sponsorship for a given purpose, and the sponsor's writing and submittal of a recommendation, to the final appointment of the candidate to a new position and the enforcement of guaranty thereafter. . . .

One is impressed with the quantity of paper that must have been consumed in the process of promoting one man and checking on the results of the promotion; yet the elaborate process was no doubt necessary if the twin dangers of blind routine and bias were to be avoided. But could the mass of information be measured by standards both fair and effective? Could the individual judgment that gave recommendation its real value be preserved in an undertaking of these proportions, or would human intelligence and character be somehow lost in the maze of forms and rules? . . .

Perhaps the first of all considerations was that of the sponsor's personal qualities. These received a degree of emphasis that was characteristically Confucian, being considered by many statesmen far more important than the institutional restraints which to us might seem more reliable. Only the selection of excellent sponsors could hope to bring about the recommendation of first class men, it was held. . . .

The most important of the sponsor's qualities was his moral character, since "only the straight know the straight." As moral qualities were the primary consideration in the candidate, they were necessarily so in the sponsor. And a good sponsor might, at least, act with greater freedom from partisanship. But how could moral qualities be ascertained? The perception of the highest worth was clearly a matter of subjective judgment not susceptible to rules. Rules could merely protect against the worst mistakes. One might consider the factors of past merit ratings, clearly demonstrable achievements, past legal offenses, or the previous requirement of discipline. The records of men previously recommended by a potential sponsor might be appraised according to criteria of varying objectivity. But all these tests yielded at best uncertain results. For positive assurance, it was necessary that the sponsors be selected as individuals and by individuals.

It was of course realized that moral worth by itself did not guarantee the ability to discern character. As Wang An-shih once wrote, he who could detect the specious man was indeed sage. Such perspicacity was recognized to be a rather rare quality, and those who possessed it left lasting reputations. Sponsors with this quality, again, were to be obtained only through personal and individual selection. . . .

The sponsor's knowledge of the candidate's qualities would be a natural consideration. The administrative relation of a sponsor to the man recommended, therefore, became of consequence. The candidate who had served under the sponsor's jurisdiction—not necessarily immediate— had greater difficulty in concealing his true character. . . .

The need that the candidate be impartially and justly selected, on the other hand, might in some ways suggest policies quite opposed to those which would promote the sponsor's knowledge of the man's qualities. The chances of impartiality might be somewhat greater in the case of a sponsor who had retired from active service, and selection might be less often motivated by personal preference when a sponsor was not formerly or prospectively in the same administrative unit as the protégé. If the sponsor were not the immediate superior of the candidate and not too close in rank, the chances either of personal friendship or rivalry might be lessened. . . . The larger the number of sponsors, the greater was the likelihood that personal prejudices would cancel out. The danger of factional power monopoly suggested in particular that the sponsors should not be limited to those who held the highest governmental posts, or to their friends, as Sung statesmen did not fail to point out. The personal selection of sponsors by the highest officials, according to subjective criteria, was for this reason clearly a hazardous practice.

When we consider the conflicting demands of the above desiderata in selecting the sponsor, it is not difficult to guess that unsatisfactory compromises and vacillating policies often emerged from the attempt to reconcile them. Objective criteria were applied widely, and a considerable diversity of devices resulted. . . .

We are told that [the emperor] T'ai-tsung in his moments of leisure examined the registers of the Secretariat-Chancellery, the Han-lin academicians, the Secretariat

special drafting officials, and the censors, seeking out those of good reputation whom he would then call to be sponsors. . . . In more of the recorded instances, however, such personal selection of sponsors was placed in the hands of a limited group of the highest officials. . . . After 1010, the growth of regular annual recommendations, permitted according to rank and office, seems to have relegated personally selected sponsors to a secondary role. . . .

In setting desirable qualifications of this kind for the prospective sponsor, the principal difficulties appear to have lain in the need to reconcile the requirements of anti-factionalism and justice with other conflicting considerations. To counterbalance the possible partiality of sponsors representing the faction in power, and to make sponsorship equally available to deserving and capable men in all parts of the service, it was desirable that the recommending power be spread widely and among officials of comparatively low rank. High officials ought not to be the sole sponsors, and perhaps should not be sponsors at all, since the administration of the system lay in their hands. This consideration also suggested the elimination from among the sponsors of those specially charged with personnel administration. But there were many arguments for the contrary policy of favoring higher officials: the desirability of choosing sponsors with greater experience, responsibility, and demonstrated ability, and very possibly that of avoiding personal friendship or rivalry as potential sources of bias. . . .

The qualifications actually applied represented an intermediate course. Sponsors were drawn in general from the upper group of the administrative class, the court officials [who held also the most important provincial posts]. While this group from the beginning numbered hundreds, and later passed the thousand mark, it constituted only perhaps a fifth to a tenth of the whole civil service. Since, however, the major factional divisions were [until 1067] represented within this group, and found their chief spokesmen there, its recommendations would not promote any single clique so long as the power was widely distributed within the group. . . .

With the codifying proclamation of 1010, the selection of sponsors was subject to more regular definition. All court officials, possibly excluding some of the highest, had both the privilege and the obligation to recommend one man each year, but not more than one. . . . All officials holding provincial commissions higher than that of prefectural vice-administrator, however, might recommend as many as they saw fit. . . .

The emphasis on recommendation by circuit and prefectural officials served a double purpose. It was valuable not only as a way of distributing selections more widely in the civil service; it also gained as sponsors men experienced in local administration, familiar with the qualities of the average subordinate official in the prefectures and subprefectures. . . .

Once the sponsors were selected, if they were all men of true worth, the act of recommendation could be left safely to their judgment, and the men they recommended could be confidently invested with responsible office. This was the ideal toward which the system aimed; but as we have already seen, it was tacitly recognized by most that the ideal was not fully realizable in practice, since one dealt not with individuals but thousands. Because the selection of sponsors of uniformly high quality could not be ensured, it was necessary to encourage those selected to make proper use of their recommending authority, and punish them for the misuse of it. . . .

The early Sung personnel administrators applied [persuasion] in the typically Confucian form of exhortations and appeals to principle, and also through rewards and commendations. . . .

While the Confucian ideal stressed [persuasion] as the only means that could win the fullest administrative responsibility in the long run, it of course acknowledged the necessary place of punishments in the practical scheme of administration. Early Sung legislation reduced considerably the severity of T'ang punishments . . . but in terms of modern concepts Sung laws were still severe.

This severity was apparent in the legal responsibility which attached to the act of sponsorship. This responsibility in a sense made the sponsor one with the man he recommended. If the candidate offended, the sponsor, even without will to offend or knowledge of the offense, became a participant in the same offense. . . .

The legal responsibility of the sponsor resembled that of the financial surety in the fact that the responsibility was voluntarily accepted. . . . But the Chinese concept of guaranty, particularly in governmental matters, involved certain connotations quite foreign to normal modern Occidental usage. To begin with, the sponsor as surety did not merely guarantee to produce the person of his candidate—the principal—in case of legal prosecution, nor did he guarantee the performance of any other single act: he guaranteed the official actions of the principal as a whole. The punishment of the principal for an offense did not end the legal responsibility of the surety: the latter was still liable to punishment, having himself become an offender. . . .

In the aspects of sponsorship that we have considered thus far, *the role of the man sponsored* has been in general a passive one: he was selected because of qualities he possessed, for the sake of performance which might reasonably be expected from him in the future on the basis of past showing. If he failed to fulfill the requirements of his new post, the blame was placed on his sponsor and perhaps on sponsorship methods through which he was selected.

Obviously, however, the performance of the sponsored man was not solely a matter of his ability and character. His effectiveness, like that of all members of the civil service, was influenced by pressures both aiding and inhibiting his desire to act in the government's interest, and by conditions which affected his morale both positively and negatively. Demands of family and friendship could conflict with those of the state. His enthusiasm could be affected by pay, working conditions, recognition, and hope of advancement. But the fact that he had been sponsored set him somewhat apart in the service, as a man in whom higher morale was to be expected. . . . Sponsorship had given him not only recognition and promotion, but the anticipation of further success in the future. The quality of his work, good or bad, was now under closer observation. If he proved efficient and scrupulous, the rules of sponsorship provided that after a term of service his case would receive special consideration for further rapid advancement. If he failed, on the other hand, the ignominy of transfer to "a distant, rustic, and lethargic place" was not a pleasant prospect. He had every reason to exert himself. . . .

The sponsored candidate had a special position in another respect also. His obligation to the men who sponsored him placed him under pressures which might be both beneficial and noxious. . . . While the state might hope to avoid prior factional ties and their damage to objective recommendation, it was almost inevitable that the act of recommendation would itself create new ties which might be factional. The man recommended would subsequently find it hard to be fully objective and impartial in his official relationships with the sponsor. . . .

CONCLUSION

What had been [the] real significance [of sponsorship?]. Certainly it had been a remarkable and unique endeavor to increase responsibility in the civil service: responsibility in the act of appointing and promoting officials, and responsible conduct on the part of the officials appointed and promoted. The play of personal influence had been brought into the open, and subjected to rules and standards. The Chinese had long recognized not only that patronage was inevitable, but that it offered

actual advantages when practiced with the interests of the state in mind. Long before the Sung that concept had been incorporated into political institutions; the task of the Sung was to expand and develop it further into a vital part of the civil service system. In the running argument between the partisans of a government of laws and those of a government of men, it afforded a ground of compromise, providing a place for both personal judgment and impersonal equity.

The method of competitive examination offered a way of testing abstract reasoning powers and skills that could be formally taught, but it could not foretell how a man would meet the practical challenges that faced an official. Merit ratings attempted to measure energy, zeal, and ability in the actual performance of duties, but were almost inevitably deficient in objectivity. Sponsorship, however, gave greater emphasis to the act of appraising merit, and strengthened the incentives to perform it objectively and responsibly. Thus sponsorship seemed particularly suited to supply the deficiencies of the examination method. . . .

How should we evaluate the practical success of sponsorship in attaining its objective? Even after a much more thorough exploration of the political life of this period than has here been possible, one could scarcely hope to isolate the influence of sponsorship from that of other factors and conditions affecting the civil service. But it is at least clear that among these various influences sponsorship was one of the more important and had much to do with the outcome.

Among the most conspicuous complaints concerning officials of this period were the low morale and venality, particularly in the lower ranks, traceable in large measure to inadequate pay. Were sponsored men freer than the average from these defects, as they should have been? We find no answer. As always, contemporary observers were voluble about abuses and shortcomings that affected them adversely; but when or if the system gave a reasonable degree of satisfaction they found no cause for comment.

We have noted the relation between sponsorship and the problem of factionalism at several points. . . . The evidence . . . seems sufficient to establish the fact that sponsorship did in some ways promote factionalism. The effects, however, were discernably of two kinds: the effect on the growth of factional groupings in general, and that on the balance of influence between the different factions.

On the one hand, it seems unlikely that the attempts to make recommendations factionally impartial were ever completely successful, and if a candidate were chiefly sponsored by a given faction, his ties to it would be further strengthened. On the other hand, the fairly wide distribution of the recommending power would tend to spread the benefits among different factions, and the favor shown to local sponsors, often men out of favor at the capital, might even weigh the balance against the stronger faction. To the extent that appointments to office were automatically governed by fixed numbers of sponsors, sponsorship would inhibit the tendency of the party in power to extend its share of the higher offices. It is conceivable that sponsorship helped to postpone the era of single party dominance. . . .

There remains a final influence of sponsorship that can be stated more confidently: the influence on the quality of the higher government circles. In the histories of the mid-eleventh century, when the government halls of K'ai-feng were notably supplied with able and vigorous men, it is not often that one reads an important official's biography without learning that at some key point in his career he received recognition and advancement through sponsorship. The most famous of these men were not, in general, from families of great prominence. Yet through the combined action of the examination and sponsorship system, many of them reached important positions at a relatively early age.

The qualities of these men reflect the system through which they rose. Nearly all the great statesmen were also famous as writers and scholars. They were men in the humanist tradition, whose interests extended to the whole culture of their times. Practically none of them were really specialists in a single narrow aspect of government activity, such as finance or water control. In this attainment, and this limitation, they displayed not merely the influence of the examination system, but the generally accepted values of the time, which guided the operation of sponsorship as well.

Equally noteworthy was the remarkable number of influential officials that in the mid-eleventh century showed a zeal for the improvement of government according to the Confucian standards, and a dedication to their task that often courted political eclipse and adversity rather than yield a principle. We need only to think of men such as Fan Chung-yen, Pao Ch'eng, Ou-yang Hsiu, Han Ch'i, Ssu-ma Kuang, Wang An-shih, or (somewhat later) Su Shih. These men differed and sometimes conflicted, but rather through temperament and in questions of immediate method than through any basic disagreement in their ultimate objectives. Their character was of the kind that the advocates of sponsorship had proposed to encourage, and their attainment of influence was perhaps the chief evidence that sponsorship had not entirely failed in its purpose.

The Criteria of Excellence

DAVID S. NIVISON

David S. Nivison is a specialist in Chinese intellectual history and teaches at Stanford University. He deals here with a fundamental concern of Chinese statesmen which had inspired many of the experiments in recruitment which we have encountered. Was there a way in which excellence in the Confucian sense could be identified and measured? Was it too elusive to be tested by the administrative procedures of a bureaucratic government? Professor Nivison's analysis amply demonstrates that the question "The Chinese Civil Service—Career Open to Talent?" remained a challenge to Chinese thinkers and statesmen through the centuries.

Students have often been found to complain about what they are required to learn and how they are held accountable for their lessons. Often their complaints follow a time-worn pattern. But if we look behind the pattern and if the students are serious, we may find that their complaints are both penetrating and important. This has been true even in China, that land of exemplary students, where teachers were respected as nowhere else, and where the emperor himself was the chief examiner.

Let me begin by telling some stories.

I

Shortly before 1060, Ou-yang Hsiu, the early Sung historian, official and man of letters, wrote a short essay, as was often done by Chinese literary men, in the back of a particularly treasured old book from his personal library. The book was an early print, from Ssu-ch'uan, of the collected prose of the ninth-century writer Han Yü. In this essay, Ou-yang Hsiu relates that as a young man, being of a poor family, he had had no books; but, finding this book discarded in the house of a friend, he begged for it and read it with fascination, not fully understanding it but nonetheless aware of its worth. In his own time, regular, so-called "modern" prose (*shih wen*) was preferred over the free style or "ancient" prose (*ku wen*) of Han Yü. "People who were skilled in it," writes Ou-yang Hsiu, "passed the examinations and were the only persons who had any reputation; no one ever talked about the writings of Han Yü." Just at this time, Ou-yang Hsiu himself had attempted the examinations unsuccessfully, and this failure had strengthened his dissatisfaction with the literary standards of his age. "I took my copy of Han Yü," he continues, "and, rereading it, I sighed and said, 'Scholars ought to go no farther than this!' And I marveled that people of the present day were so misguided." Admitting to himself that he must study for the examinations now, to obtain an official position and so be able to support his parents, he never-

Reprinted from *The Confucian Persuasion* by Arthur F. Wright, Editor, with the permission of the publishers, Stanford University Press. © 1960 by the Board of Trustees of the Leland Stanford Junior University.

theless had resolved that after he had succeeded he would turn back to what he really valued. "Later," Ou-yang Hsiu continues, "learned men throughout the world all turned their attention gradually to the past, and Han Yü's writings eventually became well known. Thirty-odd years have passed since that time, and people now study nothing but Han Yü."

Ou-yang Hsiu clearly feels that his values as a young student were right and the officially sanctioned and conventionally approved ones wrong, and that he has been vindicated, inevitably, by time. Furthermore, he is able to assure himself, his pursuit of learning has been motivated only by the purest interest in learning itself—"It was simply that I was devoted to the past," he says—and not by hope of fame or material advantage. In him, as in other Confucians of his time, conservatism, a love of antiquity, is actually a protest against an ignoble conventionality. But did not Ou-yang Hsiu capitulate? He did study for the examinations, and with conspicuous success. Further, he did this, as he admits, precisely in order to qualify for a salaried official post. The intensity of this conflict, between devotion to higher ideals and the practical necessity of coming to terms with the world, can be seen in the fact that the ultimate Confucian social duty, that of filial piety, had to be invoked to set matters right.

Yet the reasonableness of the appeal can hardly be gainsaid. It is indeed the duty of a Confucian to provide for his parents; and so here is another conflict, now between two values, both of which were Confucian: one social, one intellectual; on the one hand family duty, on the other one's own personal development.

It will be instructive to turn, for a slightly different sort of case, to the early part of the T'ang period, when the modern examination system first became important. The historian Liu Chih-chi in the early eighth century wrote, in an autobiographical essay in his *Shih T'ung* ("General Principles of History"), that when he was a child it had

been determined that he should specialize in the third of the Confucian Classics, the *Shang Shu.* But, he writes, "I was always bothered by the difficulty of its language, and . . . although I was frequently beaten, I got nowhere in my study. But when I happened to hear my father teaching my elder brothers the *Spring and Autumn Annals* and the *Commentary of Tso,* I always put aside my books and listened . . . and sighing to myself, I said, 'If only all books were like this, I would no longer be lazy!'" Liu's father was surprised at his son's independence of inclination, and, surprisingly, relented; Liu was allowed to read the *Tso Chuan,* and finished his study of it rather quickly. But now, his father would have him specialize in the *Tso Chuan* alone, going on to read all the existing commentaries to that text. To understand the father's point of view, we need to be aware that an intense study of one or two Classics served a man well in the T'ang examinations: the *chin-shih* and *ming-ching* examinations were probably the two most frequently taken even in Liu's time; and in offering for the first of these, one had to prepare one Classic, and be prepared further to find the questions dealing with commentaries rather than with the text itself. For the latter, one had to prepare somewhat less intensively in two or three Classics.

But although his father's wishes in view of this situation may have been sensible, Liu fought free again. He had wanted to read the *Tso,* not because it was an examination text but because it was history; he now wanted to read more history—not because it would get him somewhere but because it was interesting, and because he thought he had insights into it worth having. Eventually he turned aside from his interests for a few years to learn to write in the poetry and essay forms required in the examinations. He does not indicate that he was bitter about this interruption, but he makes it perfectly plain that it was an interruption in his work.

Both Liu Chih-chi and Ou-yang Hsiu,

it is evident, found themselves as young men pursuing conflicting goals. The interest of Ou-yang's and Liu's experience and of their attitudes toward it would be slight, if this experience and these attitudes were unique; but we shall see that, far from being unique, they are so common among Chinese writers of the past thousand years as to seem stereotyped. . . .

Wang Yang-ming, in the year 1518, wrote a letter of advice to two young men who were preparing for the examinations:

Since your home is poverty-stricken and your parents are old, what else can you do but seek emolument and official position? If you seek emolument and official position without studying for the examinations, you will not be able to carry out your duties as men, and will pointlessly find fault with fate. This is hardly right. But if you can firmly fix your aim, in all your pursuits fully express the Tao, and be influenced in thought neither by desire for success nor by fear of failure, then, though you study for the degree, this will be no real hindrance to your learning to become virtuous men.

Wang, like Ou-yang Hsiu, here justifies the pursuit of worldly ends by appeal to the obligation of *filial duty*. There is more, of course, to Wang's attitude than this. He reveals himself highly suspicious of the influence the examinations had on a young man's mind. It may be possible, he reluctantly concedes, for a man to study for the degree of *chü-jen* or *chin-shih* without detriment to his self-development; all too many, however, through "lack of a fixed aim," as Wang puts it, "have come to think exclusively of honor, gain and literary style"; and as a result "they cannot avoid cherishing the desire for small advantages and quick results." A young man must always resist this temptation the examinations present to him to succumb to vulgar values and to let his desires be involved in what he is doing. . . .

II

The civil service examinations have been called the hallmark of the "Confucian state." Preparing for them in order to seek an official career was a basic duty to family and to the world. Their existence as an institution more than anything else signalized the ascendancy of the man of learning and culture in society. Yet, almost from the beginnings of this institution in the later empire, the examinations, and the educational standards they produced, were resented and criticized. Students resented being fettered and constrained. Statesmen found the institution wanting as a means of "nurturing talent" and recruiting the best men for public service. Literary critics and moral philosophers bewailed its influence on the quality of letters and on the state of public and private virtue. This polyphony of protest may be found in every generation. And the surprising fact is that throughout all this we find the examination-education complex, the function and effect of which was to ensure the dominance of the Confucian classical tradition, criticized precisely by appeal to *Confucian* moral, aesthetic, and political values.

This is not a situation we would have expected. Its oddity may help to explain the fact that, for all of the attention scholars have given to the imperial examination system and its ramifications, the long tradition of protest against this system has been almost completely ignored. In what follows I shall attempt to open the matter up. My attempt will of necessity be extremely superficial, for the volume of relevant literature is enormous: in this literature we must include innumerable personal letters and essays, novels (such as *Ju-lin Wai-shih* by Wu Ching-tzu, 1701–54) on the life of the literati, as well as many official and unofficial treatises on public policy. Simply to relate the history of reforms and proposed changes in the system would require volumes. But an analysis of some of the ideals and motivations which perpetually generated this criticism may be more feasible.

The motive of Liu Chih-chi's self-assertion was his wish to pursue an easily comprehended interest—namely, in history and in the traditions of historical writing; and for this interest he has little compulsion to offer any further justification (though there is ample Confucian justification for it). With Ou-yang Hsiu the case is different. He admired the writing of Han Yü, yes; but this was not all. He was also "devoted to the past," and he scorned present-day styles, mastery in which served others in the mere pursuit of gain. We are inclined to ask, On behalf of just what ideals is this disinterestedness urged? Ou-yang Hsiu does not say, but it is fair to note that this very disinterestedness, the claim that the quest for gain and fame for oneself is unworthy of a writer, is itself an ideal of a higher order. Why should it seem appropriate to Ou-yang Hsiu to link this attitude with an esteem for Han Yü?

The reason may be that Han Yü has given this ideal for the literary man in China perhaps its most beautiful and intensely moving expression. In a letter "In Reply to Li I," Han, for the benefit of his correspondent (who apparently had asked questions about literary art, and perhaps had sent some writings), describes his own earlier efforts to learn to write. . . .

The task of learning to write is not at all one of learning verbal tricks and forms; it is a task of self-cultivation, a *moral* exercise, a matter of nourishing one's *ch'i* or spirit; *ch'i* is like water, words the mere objects that "float" in it; if *ch'i* is adequate, there will be no trouble with words. This literary ideal is found everywhere in Chinese critical thought since T'ang . . . and has had the effect of making literary criticism in China a variety of moral philosophy. "If you hope to grasp the ancient ideal of writing," Han tells his reader, "then do not hope for quick success, do not be tempted by power and advantage; nourish your roots and wait for the fruit; add the oil and wait for the light . . ."

A person who does this will come close to perfection. But, Han stresses, he will be largely unappreciated; he will "seldom be used by others," i.e., employed by those in power. Setting out to be a good writer is not to be advertised as a good way to get a position. Han closes by saying that it is just because he realizes his friend is not interested in "gain" that he is willing to speak to him frankly. "If you wait to be employed by others, you will be like a mere utensil; your being used or neglected will depend on others. The superior man is not like this. In ordering his mind, he has the Tao. In conducting himself, he is upright." Rank and position mean nothing to him. "When he is employed, he applies his Tao to others. When he is unemployed, he transmits it to his disciples, commits it to writing and creates a model for later generations."

For anyone taking Han's view of writing really seriously, it is difficult to see how studying for the literary examinations—deliberately seeking the road to "gain" and preferment—could be anything but a stumbling block on the path of self-cultivation. And we should notice in particular how Han Yü associates not only writing, but also teaching, with indifference to mundane success or failure. The good man does not seek office. If it comes his way, he does his best. If it does not, he writes and teaches. In both modes of life he serves and is devoted to the Tao.

But was the literary and moral ideal expressed in the letter to Li I actually related in this way to the problem of the examinations in Han Yü's mind? Han has answered this question explicitly in a letter to another friend named Ts'ui Li-chih.

At the time of writing, Han had for the second time failed to obtain office through the placing examinations offered under the Board of Civil Office, and Ts'ui had written to urge him not to lose heart. Han replied with a long *apologia*:

When I was sixteen or seventeen, I had no knowledge of the realities of the world. I read the books of the sages, and thought to myself that when a man enters official service, he is acting only for others with no advantage for himself. When I reached twenty, I was distressed by the poverty of my household; I consulted with members of my family and came to understand that official service is not just to the advantage of persons other than oneself.

Han went to the capital, noted that men who became *chin-shih* were highly honored, and set out eagerly to acquire the skill to become one of them. He was shown examples of questions that had been used in the examinations administered by the Board of Ceremonies—calling for pieces of rhymed prose, poetry, and essays, and considered that he could write these things without studying, so he tried at the examinations; but the examiners' standards were purely subjective: Han tried four times before succeeding, and even then was not given a post. Following this he tried twice at the placing examination, excited by the idea of the fame he would gain by passing —though he noticed with surprise when he looked at successful essays that they were of just the kind required by the Board of Ceremonies. He set to work, like an actor learning his lines, for several months; again, however, he was disappointed in his quest for office.

Then, Han says, he took stock of himself, and realized that the standards he was following and those of the examiners were utterly different. If Ch'ü Yüan, Mencius, and Ssu-ma Ch'ien were to find themselves competing for these honors they would be ashamed; they simply would not push themselves forward in this way;

but if they did take part in this abysmal competition, they would surely fail. Yet, if these men were living today, though their Tao were not recognized by the world, would this shake their confidence? Would they be willing to have their worth decided in competition with mere time-servers by the rating of one dunce of an examiner, and be pleased or distressed at his decision?

Han then realized that the most he could hope to gain from success in the examinations would be advantages of a paltry material sort.

He concluded by assuring Ts'ui (and himself) that he was not (as Ts'ui had suggested) to be compared to Pien Ho in Han Fei-tzu's story, who had twice tendered his "uncut jade" to the King of Ch'u only to have a foot cut off on each attempt. He has offered no "jade" to his ruler—yet. But he can. The times are troubled; the world has fallen short of ancient ideals; the dynasty is militarily insecure; the emperor and his ministers are worried; Han can analyze these difficulties and offer his views. Perhaps he will be recognized and rewarded with a high post; but if not, Han said, he can tend his sequestered plot in quietness, and search out the details of the history of the dynasty, the lives of its great men, and write a "classic" on the T'ang, which will condemn villains and sycophants and praise examples of concealed virtue. This he will pass on to posterity forever.

A really good man, apparently, is above playing the ordinary game, and will refuse to accept the judgment meted out to the many. If the court has the wisdom to use him, good; if not, he is not hindered in his devotion to the Tao. . . .

Han's concern with the examinations in relation to his own literary ideals suggests that in his time the examination system was an active political issue. This seems indeed to have been the case. In the later T'ang empire, . . . profound (and as yet inadequately understood) social changes were taking place. The great aristocratic families of the north, which had been powerful in an earlier era, were declining or breaking up, and "new men" from outside this closed elite were coming on the scene. The availability of office to members of different social or regional groups was therefore a matter of intense interest, and the question was raised whether the examinations brought into office men who truly deserved it.

A prominent criticism was that the examinations rewarded the man who merely happened to have a good memory, though he might have no grasp of the "essential meaning" of the Classics—their relevance to current moral and political issues. Another persistent issue was the propriety of requiring of the candidate a facility in highly artificial literary forms such as the *fu* ("rhymed prose") and *p'an* ("decision") which could have nothing to do with his performance in office. Yüan Chen in 806, for example, in an essay submitted at the Palace Examination, made a revolutionary proposal that chief emphasis in the examinations be placed on knowledge of contemporary law and history, and that the competition be opened to all ranks of society (he would have abolished the examination on which Han Yü foundered, the placing examination, which required a candidate to prove that his father was neither an artisan, nor a merchant, nor a criminal).

But such criticisms do not question the value of the examination system in principle. One important kind of criticism did do just this. Curiously, we find this criticism brought out with special clarity in a somewhat backhanded justification of the literary requirements. This appears in the "Monograph on Examinations" of the *Hsin T'ang Shu*. The authors observe that although in the *chin-shih* examination "the choice is made on the basis of literary compositions written in a vague style and on subjects of little practical value," still the successful candidates do perform well in office. They continue:

In later ages (i.e., after classical antiquity), customs became more and more corrupted, and superiors and inferiors came to suspect each other. Hence it came to be thought that the correctness of a candidate's use of rimes would allow examiners to judge his merits objectively. Whenever this procedure was abandoned, . . . no stable standard could be established. And consequently, it has never been possible to change anything. Alas, it is clear therefore that the method used in the Three Dynasties of antiquity, whereby local districts presented men to the sovereign because of their virtuous conduct, is one which cannot obtain except under a perfect government.

Here eleventh-century historians are picking up ideas from a proposal made in 763 to "restore" certain features of a system for the direct recommendation of "virtuous" men to the court. Nonetheless, they are editorializing; and we might bear in mind that the editor who directed the compilation of this part of the *Hsin T'ang Shu*— in all probability writing parts of it himself—was Ou-yang Hsiu.

The idea of doing away with the examinations entirely, and of filling the ranks of government servants by recommendation of "virtuous" men from below, was resurrected again and again.[1] It bears witness to an almost incredible extreme of political idealism in Sung and Ming China. The vision was of a perfect society supposed to have existed in antiquity, a government of perfect virtue, in which there would be complete mutual trust and harmony between men of high and low estate. Inferiors would know their station and have no desire to rise beyond their merits, while those above would be motivated only by the purest love of virtue itself. In such a world order, the best man would always be chosen (and those not chosen would have no resentment), for it would always be the best who would come to the attention of the rulers, and the rulers would always be able to recognize the best. Examinations would not only be superfluous in such a state of affairs, they would be incompatible with it, for they would excite a spirit of striving and of selfish competition among the people. This is just what the examinations do; and for many Sung and Ming philosophers this corrupting and disturbing influence exercised upon the mind, preventing men from "fixing their aim" on ultimate moral values instead of short-term gains, is the greatest fault of the system.

The utopian picture of an ancient, prebureaucratic, perfect Confucian society was

---

[1] This idea, basically a piece of Confucian feudal utopianism, should not be confused with the system of promotion by recommendation actually in use in the Sung period. The Sung recommendation device, as Kracke makes clear, was essentially a means of promoting and assigning officials rather than a means of recruitment into the civil service.

a basic element underlying and shaping opinion about educational policy and examination practices in the factional politics of the Sung; indeed this utopian conception seems to be central in all reformist and counterreformist thought in that period. Here I cannot take up the details of these policy struggles, save to note that these questions were always important. Examination requirements were changed constantly, and this must have resulted in much anxiety, leading in turn to an intensification of concern over these problems. Basically, the call for ending the examinations and turning back to some earlier and presumably better method of bringing good men into government—easily combined with a Mencius-inspired concern for the reform of local schools—was of a piece with Mencian "well-field" utopianism in economics and land policy. Essentially it was part of an idealistic regret that the "Confucian" bureaucratic state, with its contamination of Legalism and its (real or fancied) attendant moral corruption in official life, had come into existence at all.

Two illustrations will bear this out, both from Sung philosophers of first rank. Ch'eng I (1033–1107), in a long discussion of examinations as conducted in the "three colleges" of the Sung Imperial Academy, expressed the usual regrets: the formal, detailed, legally prescribed literary requirements were not of use in evaluating the moral worth of the students, while the atmosphere of competition turned their minds to a love of "profit," and made them actually forget their parents. The trouble is that the government relies on "detailed regulations" for appraising candidates for the civil service, rather than on whatever ability those in high places may have to recognize "virtue." But are "detailed regulations" really dispensable?

Someone may say, "If the right men are obtained for the highest positions, then all is well. But if not, it is better to have many detailed regulations to guard against wrongdoing, so that there will be a clear course to follow." Such a person fails entirely to realize

that the ancient rulers devised laws in the expectation that there would be suitable men to carry them out. I have never heard that they made laws for the case in which capable men could not be found. If the high officials are not good men, and do not understand the principle of education, but merely adhere to the empty letter and the minute details of the law, surely they will not be able by these means to lead men to perfect their talents.

Ch'eng's reply is a standard Confucian rejoinder to quasi-Legalist recipes: the law cannot effect its own implementation; at best it is a guide for the judgment of good men.

But Ch'eng did not proceed very far with these anti-bureaucratic regrets. Another philosopher, Chang Tsai (1020–77), however, was so repelled by the spectacle of vulgar competition for positions that he praised, in contrast, the giving and holding of hereditary offices, which had persisted in the later bureaucratic empire as a not very significant and rather artificial continuation of ancient feudal forms.

The distinction of hereditary office is the way a ruler gives recognition to those who achieve great things and honors the virtuous, cherishing them and being generous to them, displaying his boundless grace. Their heirs therefore ought to be happy with their duties and be encouraged to achievement . . . excelling in purity and abstaining from the pursuit of profit.

But in these times, Chang complained, "descendants of high dignitaries like to compete with ordinary people, working at the craft of verse-making and selling their wares to the authorities," i.e., sitting for the examinations in the hope of getting appointments, "not realizing that actively seeking for office is wrong."

Chang Tsai's feeling that it is unseemly for a man of quality to engage in the common scramble for advantage is here perhaps reinforced by another persuasion: that the gentleman will not push himself forward. This is the conduct one expects of a social climber; the true "superior man" waits until his prince calls him. But this is not for excess of humility; on the contrary, he may be deeply offended if it be thought that his merits are open to question. An amusing story told of "the philosopher Ch'eng" (either Ch'eng I or his brother Ch'eng Hao, 1032–85) shows how ingrained these attitudes were.

Hsieh Chi passed through Loyang on his way from Shu to the capital and saw Ch'eng-tzu. The master asked him, "Why have you undertaken this trip?" He answered, "I am about to take the examination for a post in the Bureau of Education." The master did not reply. Chi said, "What do you think of it?" The master said, "Once when I was buying a servant-girl I wanted to test her. Her mother became angry and would not permit it, saying, 'My daughter is not one who may first be tried out.' Today you want to become a teacher of men and want to undergo a test for this purpose! You would certainly be laughed at by that old woman." Chi subsequently did not go.

Dignity is a precious thing indeed! Clearly, a dignified and lofty refusal to compete, a high-minded protest that one is not interested in advancement and will leave this matter to fate, and the cherishing of a picture of society in which the poisonous craving for "profit" is absent, are all attitudes which fit closely together.

In considering the bearing of Neo-Confucian ethical thought upon the examination problem, we cannot neglect the most famous of Sung philosopher-statesmen, Chu Hsi (1130–1200). Chu, describing the idealized ancient practice of recruiting officials by direct recommendation without examinations, says that as a result of it "men's minds were composed and they had no distracting desires. Night and day they were diligent, fearing only lest they be wanting in virtue, and not caring whether rank and salary came their way." Clearly he too shared the common Neo-Confucian nostalgic utopian ideal.

Chu Hsi made the foregoing statement in an essay which in its day was famous— a "Private Opinion on Schools and Ex-

aminations," which, the "Monograph on Examinations" in the *Sung Shih* tells us, "was read by the whole world." In it he was bitterly critical of examination standards and practices in his day. He proposed at least a limited use of direct recommendation, and an end to practices of favoritism; in particular he called for fairer geographical distribution when allocating quotas of candidates to be passed. The main part of his proposal, however, would have had the effect of making the examinations very different in content and tone: he would change the subject matter of the examinations through a twelve-year cycle, guaranteeing that the state would have at its disposal men with a wide variety of specialized backgrounds. Examinations in poetry and *fu* would be suppressed. Chu wanted his candidates to think, and to know how to think for themselves; in studying the Classics, they should study not only the classical texts but also the commentaries of different schools of interpreters, and in answering a question should be prepared to cite different opinions, concluding with their own judgment. Chu went on actually to list commentaries he would have examinees required to read; somewhat surprisingly, commentaries by Wang An-shih are included for all the most important Classics, although Chu was in general opposed to Wang's policies. Chu expected much if his proposals were acted upon. If they were adopted, "men's minds would be composed and there would be no spirit of hustling and striving; there would be actual virtuous conduct and none of the corruption of empty words; there would be solid learning and no unusable talent."

Chu in this essay was flailing away at the system, and doing so, at least in part, in terms of his ideal of a perfect social and political order. But this ideal of a perfectly virtuous world was ambiguous. It could be used, not to criticize the edifice of requirements, standards, pressures, or unfair practices which confronted the student, but rather to upbraid the student himself. For one can say that in a perfectly virtuous society the government would not make the mistakes the examination system embodied; but, by the same argument, students would not exhibit the qualities of restless self-seeking and anxiety that these mistakes induced. Chu has a rather often-quoted remark that "it is not that the examinations are a vexation to men, but simply that men vex themselves about the examinations." And he continues,

A scholar of lofty vision and broad understanding, when he reads the books of the sages, will produce writing which reflects what he grasps, and all considerations of gain and loss, advantage and disadvantage, are set aside. Even though he constantly works at preparing for the examinations, he is undisturbed. If Confucius were to come back to life now, he would not avoid the examinations; but surely they would not disturb him.

. . . Chu says that he himself as a young man found examination studies naturally distasteful to him, but argues that this natural disinclination was of no significance. The plain implication in this is that Chu was approached by unhappy students who also found their examination studies distasteful, who felt that the guidance of their own inclinations was valuable, and who found themselves, like Ou-yang Hsiu and Liu Chih-chi, inclined to spend their time on other lines of study and self-improvement. Chu is shown by the *Ch'üan Shu* editors to have dealt with this plaint in various ways. Sometimes he simply pooh-poohs all the fuss about the matter:

Concerning study for the examinations, there is really nothing very important to be said. When a man of worth devotes himself to it, he will presumably have some energy to spare. If he has understood the true philosophy, then in the course of his daily activities, whatever their degree of importance, he will not need to divide his attention: if he always first understands "this," he will succeed at "that."

In other words, see that you cultivate yourself properly and study the right point of view, and there will be no conflict—you

will automatically do well in the examinations. As Han Yü had said, a good man will naturally write well. Chu's friend and rival philosopher Lu Chiu-yüan picked up the same idea when, in 1181, he was guest lecturer at Chu's White Deer Grotto Academy. Cultivate yourself circumspectly, says Lu, instill in yourself a devotion to right, and learn to have no impulses toward selfish expediency. "When one who conducts himself in this way approaches the examination halls, his writing will always express the learning and self-cultivation in which he is constantly engaged and the richness stored up within himself, and he will not offend against the sages.". . .

Chu recognizes the common rationalization of students that they must study for the examinations in order to support their parents, and he condemns it. Such an attitude merely indicates that the student's mind is not composed—that he still feels a conflict between studying for the examinations and "real learning." Sometimes, however, Chu admits by implication that there can be such a conflict, and attempts to deal with it or resolve it by some argument or stratagem. On one occasion, a disciple named Huang Ch'ien was ordered by his father to go to the prefectural school and study for the examinations, a course the young student was much disinclined to take. Huang laid his situation before Chu, who replied, "You can study for the examinations in the daytime and read the books you want to at night!" and added that if Huang refused to follow his father's wishes, father and son would become estranged, a situation which, he implies, would be as detrimental to Huang's program of "study" (i.e., self-cultivation) as the examinations course could ever be.

As we might expect, Wang Yang-ming shared the Neo-Confucian vision of a perfect, strife-free society. Writing in 1525, he gives this idyllic picture of antiquity:

The man at the village well or in the rural district, the farmer, the artisan, the merchant, everybody had this (the true) learning . . .

and looked only to the perfecting of character as important. How is this to be accounted for? They were not subject to the confusion inherent in much hearing and seeing, nor to the annoyance of remembering and reciting, nor to extravagance of speech and composition, nor to the striving and gaining of honor and advantage. The result was that they were filial toward their parents, respectful to their elders, and faithful toward their friends.

In this remote age, "the government schools were devoted to perfecting virtue, . . ." and "the people of the empire, with clear, resplendent virtue, all viewed one another as relatives of one home. . . . They did not strive for exalted position," each being content with his station. People at this time were not envious of others' accomplishments: "They did not distinguish between themselves and others. . . . They can be compared with the body of a single person . . ." and as one's eyes are not ashamed because they cannot hear, likewise no man was ashamed or was thought ill of for lack of the intellectual attainments found in the great.

If this is noteworthy, it is chiefly as an intense (if dreamy) re-expression of a common Neo-Confucian political ideal. It is obvious, at least, that the addition of an examination system would seriously mar Wang's pretty scene. If there is a novel emphasis in what he says, it is found in his almost Taoist feeling that the purity of men's minds will be injured by too much "seeing and hearing," "remembering and reciting," or by "extravagance of speech and composition." For it is typical of Wang that he has a rather wholesale distrust of the verbal, conceptual side of man's mental existence. His distrust of mere "words" fits into a growing intellectual trend which became very important in the Ch'ing.

This attitude can be more easily understood if we examine the character of the district and metropolitan examinations during the Ming (to a large extent the description will fit the Ch'ing also). The Ming examinations followed, with some modification, the form of the Sung examinations as revised in 1071 when, as a result of one of the reforms of Wang An-shih, the *ming-ching* examination was abolished and certain features of it incorporated into the *chin-shih* examination. As it ultimately took shape, the Ming examination scheme (for both *chin-shih* and *chü-jen* degrees) consisted of three sittings or tests several days apart. The first test consisted of "essays on the meaning of the Classics" (*ching-i*)—three on the Four Books, and four on texts from other Classics. The second test was given over to *lun* ("essays") and *p'an* ("decisions," a T'ang examination form) and to questions on imperial "instructions"; the third, to *ts'e* ("dissertations") on history and current problems. As far as this description goes, such an examination might be quite comprehensive. Actually, as Ku Yen-wu points out, the only test given any careful attention by the examiners was the first, on the meaning of the Classics and the Four Books. Further, although all candidates had to answer questions on the Four Books, it was possible to get by with specialization on just one other Classic. This was certainly very far from what Chu Hsi had wanted in his "Private Opinion."

But this was not all. Where Chu had wanted candidates to have a knowledge of many different schools of criticism, the Ming system required candidates to prepare themselves in the views of just one school, ironically the school of Chu Hsi himself. After the official publication, in the Yung-lo reign, of the compendium of the opinions of this school, the *Ssu-shu Wu-ching Ta-ch'üan*, even the standard T'ang commentaries were dispensed with. In consequence, less and less came to depend on wide learning or genuine understanding, even of the Classics themselves; more and more it came to be crucially important for the candidate to excel in the style of his essays on the meaning of classical texts in the first test.

What of the form of these essays? A form for the *ching-i* essay had been fixed by the Board of Ceremonies shortly after

Wang An-shih's reform; and as such official forms will, it evolved over successive reigns and dynasties. By the Ming, it had come to be fixed in eight sections (hence its popular name, *pa-ku*, "eight legs"). The number of words to be used in the essay was also fixed from time to time. A typical specimen takes the announced topic—a passage from one of the Classics—and analyzes it into two subthemes. The essay then moves into a more and more elaborate treatment of these two themes. In the main body of the essay, an extended sentence or group of sentences will be put forward on one of the themes; these are in loose, "ancient prose" style, but they are at once followed by an exactly similar sentence or set of sentences on the other theme, which mirror the earlier ones character for character. This game will be played several times before the essay reaches its close. In tone, the entire piece can effectively be compared with a sermon on a text from sacred scripture.

The total effect is not at all displeasing, if one is merely browsing through a few of these curios, and surely some value must be acknowledged in any literary form which required the Chinese literati to write well-constructed and systematically organized pieces of prose. But if one had to read and imitate such essays as if one's life depended upon it for the years needed to acquire sufficient skill to satisfy the examiners, one can readily imagine that ennui would soon give way to intense distaste. The necessity of finding antitheses in the theme in order to carry the essay through was particularly galling, since it was a purely formal requirement which took precedence over whatever meaning the classical passage might contain. Candidates had to be prepared to distort, or even invent, meaning in the assigned text, and had by long practice to learn this art thoroughly.

Worse, the examiners over the centuries not unnaturally developed a little tradition of playing a game with the candidates, by choosing texts which would be difficult to handle in the required way, or which were chopped out of context in the most misleading fashion possible, with the natural phrasing and breaks in meaning of the original text largely ignored. An example, given by Chu Hsi (who excoriated the practice in his "Private Opinion") is a Sung examination question consisting of three lines from the *Shih ching*, viz.,

> Shang t'ien chih tsai
> Wu sheng wu ch'ou
> I hsing Wen Wang

Legge's translation is as follows:

> The doings of high heaven
> have neither sound nor smell.
> Take your pattern from King Wen, . . .

The second half of the second pair of lines, which is dropped, is approximately "and all countries will give you their confidence." But of course much more context even than this would be required if one were to make sense out of the passage. Still, Chu Hsi's example is tame compared to what sometimes happened. Imagine yourself writing an essay on the following five words:

> Kou wei wu pen ch'i

These words correspond approximately to the italic words in the following passage from *Mencius*:

> The disciple Hsü said, "Chung-ni often praised water, saying, 'O water, O water.' What did he find in water to praise?" Mencius replied, "There is a spring of water; how it gushes out! It rests not day nor night. It fills up every hole, and then advances, flowing on to the four seas. Such is water having a spring! It was this which he found in it to praise.
> "*But suppose that* the water *has no spring.* —*In the seventh* and eighth months when the rain falls abundantly, the channels in the fields are all filled, but their being dried up again may be expected in a short time. So a superior man is ashamed of a reputation beyond his merits.

In the *pa-ku* as part of the examinations, clearly, we have a prime example of violation of the classical principle that "one must not let words injure meaning." The term *pa-ku* came widely to connote an exercise in mere verbal cleverness with utter disregard for content. Reflect that every schoolboy had to struggle with this form, and that often all possible social, family, and pedagogical pressure was put upon him to master it. And consider that in order to master it he had to develop by long practice at least a hypothetical sort of taste for it, and thus condition himself in a device for which he was likely to have both philosophical and aesthetic disgust. The bitter complaints about *shih wen* (this term now had come to mean *pa-ku*) in the letters and reminiscences of seventeenth- and eighteenth-century writers are not hard to understand.

Ku Yen-wu, in the seventeenth century, was one of several now famous men who meditated and wrote on the reasons for the decline and fall of the Ming Dynasty. Much of his *Jih-chih Lu* has this sort of point, and in particular the parts of that book dealing with examinations and schools, though treating these subjects in great historical depth, are pointed up into a criticism, often extremely biting, of the character and operation of the Ming examination system. In many of these critical sections, however, he writes as though he were talking of contemporary conditions, and we probably must assume that at the time he wrote conditions had not greatly changed.

Ku insists that writing, to be worth anything, must say something, and the writer must be unencumbered by formal restrictions in the saying of it:

Writing can have no fixed form. When a form is set for people to follow in their writing, the writing will not be worth talking about. The T'ang selected its officials on their skill in writing *fu*, and the *fu* became utterly decadent. The Sung selected men on their skill in composing essays and dissertations (*lun ts'e*) and these genres likewise decayed. The Ming selected men on the basis of their essays on the meaning of the Classics (*ching-i*, i.e., *pa-ku*), and this form of writing became

worse than anything that had been seen before. The reason in each case was that writing was required to follow a fixed form, and as a result the writing continually became worse. The reason the examination replies of Ch'ao Ts'o, Tung Chung-shu, and Kung-sun Hung are outstanding in history is that in their day there was no fixed form for writing. If we wish to invigorate the writing of the present day we must not fetter it with forms, and then outstanding talent will make its appearance.

In Sung, Yüan, and Ming, the characteristic objection to the examination system had been its tendency to induce a fever of competition. Ku's indictment of *pa-ku* suggests that the characteristic objection was now to the examinations' bad influence on writing and thinking. By stressing purely formal, merely verbal inducements to stagnation, the examinations actually deprived the state of a supply of good men. The situation has become so bad, Ku thinks, that the only remedy is to suspend the examinations altogether for a time, and teach people anew how to study. Ku also attacks the brainless orthodoxy which he feels the examinations propagate, and recommends that examination questions on the Four Books deal with "doubtful" matters, questions which will probe into embarrassing contradictions. Ku cites the *p'an* genre on the T'ang examinations as exemplifying what he intends, but it is likely that some of the examination questions prepared by Wang An-shih would have served him even better. Ku, however, had a rather low opinion of the Sung reformer.

Ku reserves his strongest language for a somewhat different matter, however. Just because the examinations place so much emphasis on formally correct essay writing, they do nothing to recognize or encourage really solid scholarship. Instead, the examinations are so contrived as to allow mere know-nothings to pass. Ku's exposé of the abuses by which this can occur is one of the bitterest and most interesting parts of his treatise. The trick consists of a practice Ku calls *ni t'i,* or "making up questions."

There is, he says, no evil greater than this in the whole system. It works as follows: In the crucial first test, when a candidate has to write essays on the Classics he has chosen as a specialty, there will usually be only a few dozen questions likely to be asked.

Rich families and powerful clans engage well-known scholars and install them in their family schools. The scholar then takes these few dozen themes and writes an essay for each, receiving pay according to the number of essays he writes. The sons and younger brothers in the family, and servant boys who are especially clever, are then made to memorize and study thoroughly these essays. When they go to the examination halls, eight or nine out of every ten themes announced will correspond to the themes they have studied, and they need only copy down the writings they have memorized.

This procedure, Ku observes, is incomparably easier than the examinations as they are traditionally pictured; for plainly, the son of a rich family might in this way pass without having read through the text of even one Classic. "The same procedure," Ku writes, "is used for the Four Books. And when the grades are announced, these fellows turn out to be at the top. Many who are mere pretty-faced youths are selected for official appointments."

Ku then adds that from time to time parts of the Classics have ceased to be drawn upon for examination themes, so that what a young man has to contend with in his preparation has become less and less, and the trick of "making up likely themes" becomes that much easier. As a result,

What men in former times needed ten years to accomplish can now be finished in one; what once required a year to learn can now be finished in a month. . . . But if by chance you ask someone about a Classic he has not read, there are those who will be so confused they will not know what book you are talking about. Therefore, I say that the injurious effects of *pa-ku* are as great as the effects of the Burning of the Books, and the

ruination of talent that it brings about is worse than the result of the Burial of the Scholars. . . .

Ku then recommends, citing Chu Hsi's "Private Opinion," that candidates be examined on passages in the Classics that would call for some original thinking, and that in studying one Classic they be required to gain a general acquaintance with the rest; that they be required to become familiar with conflicting interpretations, and that in their answers they be required to render their own judgment. Further, themes used in the examinations should not be so standard that they can be guessed at in advance. "Then their essays will have to be written in the examination halls, and it can really be determined whether a scholar understands the Classics or not, and his ability to write can really be tested."

Not the least interesting part of what Ku says is his conviction that it is characteristically the rich who are most easily able to get away with murder. But the substance of his plea is that solid scholarship should be demanded of a candidate at the examinations and should be the criterion of his worth. In this plea Ku perhaps had real influence, for his prestige as a classical scholar mounted enormously in the next century. Successive generations of scholars grew up who looked back to him with reverence, and many such men, of course, served frequently as examining officials. One can well imagine that one of Ku's "pretty-faced youths" would have scant chance of passing under such an examiner as, say, Juan Yüan.

But this same prestige of Ku as a classical scholar, and the philological *zeitgeist* which developed in the eighteenth century, had eventually another and very different effect on examination standards. For although the tendency occasionally improved the caliber of examining officials, still, in any given case, the chances were that an examiner would find himself in the situation of passing judgment on a candidate or candidates who knew more philology than he did.

Examiners caught in this sort of situation tend to look for a simple and foolproof line of defense into which to retreat. The examiner's recourse in the present case was to limit his inspection once again to mere questions of form: not, now, to the formal correctness of the candidate's essays, but to the form of the individual characters he wrote—to his calligraphy. By the second and third decades of the nineteenth century, it was a ritual perfection in the handling of the brush which was the mark of the candidate most likely to succeed.

Needless to say, this new situation provoked protests appropriate to it. Such an expression of protest is to be found in a bitterly sarcastic essay by Kung Tzu-chen, an intense, brilliant, and erratic scholar-official, philologist, poet, and friend of Wei Yüan and Lin Tse-hsü, who attempted the examinations repeatedly before attaining the *chin-shih* degree in 1829, failing, however—as he believed, because of poor handwriting—to pass the palace examination which a successful *chin-shih* normally took. Kung's essay pretends to be a preface to a book he has written on calligraphy. He describes first, with mock reverence, the ritual of the palace examination in which he failed. The examining officers, "in court robes, face the throne and kneel thrice, touching their heads to the floor nine times. All the candidates do likewise, respectfully taking their positions. When the examination is over, the eight examiners then respectfully make a selection of ten papers in which the elevation of characters is according to form and in which even and deflected tones have been properly used, and which exhibit a formal calligraphic style which is especially sparkling and delicate, presenting these for the emperor's perusal. . . ."

Kung describes more examinations—the preliminary examination before the palace examination, and the examination following it, both, again, turning on the candidate's skill in calligraphy. He misses no chance to dwell on the grave and weighty importance of success which turns on so trivial a matter. "Those who place high in all three examinations are appointed to the Han-lin Academy. In our dynasty, the highest officials invariably arise from among members of the Han-lin, and more than half of the assistant ministers at court and of the governors of provinces are chosen in the same way." To be chosen for a clerkship in the Grand Council is likewise a great honor; for "in time of war the function of the Grand Council is to assist the throne in making plans by which victory is decided, while in time of peace it provides advice based on the records of earlier emperors in the issuance of edicts affecting the imperial household." But, "when one is recommended to the Grand Council there is an examination, in which selection is made as before on the basis of calligraphic skill." Kung goes on to explain to us how other important posts are filled, and always with the same final twist.

Finally Kung tips his hand:

I, Kung Tzu-chen, passed the examination in the Board of Ceremonies; three times I went up for the palace examination and three times I failed. I was not assigned to the Han-lin Academy. I was examined for the Grand Council but was not given a post there. . . . So I have withdrawn to my home and have reproached myself, and have written a book in self-criticism. Its contents consist of twelve sections discussing the principles of selecting a fine brush-tip, five sections on the proper method of grinding the ink and impregnating the brush, . . . one hundred and twenty sections on fine points in the drawing of the dot and in the execution of the sweeping down-stroke, twenty-two sections on the framing of characters, twenty-four sections on the spacing of characters in column, three sections on quality of spirit; and seven sections on natural temper. Having finished the work, I have entitled it *A New Treatise on Gaining Office,* and am entrusting it to my descendants.

Kung dates his "preface" the fourteenth year of Tao-kuang (1834).

Needless to say, Kung's *Treatise* was never written or even seriously contemplated. Kung's bitterness about calligraphy, it should be stressed, was provoked by a situation peculiar to his time. We find a very different attitude in Ku Yen-wu. Ku would have his candidates know how to write characters well, and no nonsense. He cites in this connection, and with evident approval, a practice in court examinations in the Northern Ch'i Dynasty. In those high and far-off times, it seems, if a candidate's writing was sloppy, he was required as a penalty to drink a pint of ink.

The Chinese civil service examinations were not discontinued until 1905. The remainder of the story, however, would be a study in itself, and I lack both the space and the knowledge to enter upon it. But it does seem plain that it would be hasty to ascribe the Chinese state's rejection of the examination system simply to a Westernizing fever, or to say that the Chinese did away with that system merely in order to be rid of a conservative institutional force. Perhaps it will turn out that what the "impact of the West" accomplished was to tip the balance in favor of persuasions which were centuries old, but which had not been strong enough radically to alter the set institutions of a bureaucratic state. The complaint that the examinations failed to nourish talents of practical use to the state was not a new and radical idea in the nineteenth century; on the contrary, it was a familiar criticism in the ninth.

SUGGESTIONS FOR ADDITIONAL READING

As an idea and an institution, the Chinese civil service was closely intertwined with many aspects of Chinese life, political, social, economic, and cultural. Only a few relevant and suggestive works can be cited here. Literature in non-Western languages is voluminous, but is here excluded.

The structure of the Chinese government within which the civil service functioned has been studied for most dynasties. Works on the functions and organization of government contain much useful information on the civil service, but are too numerous to be listed here. They can be tracked down in some of the standard bibliographies on Chinese history and in the general bibliography that appears annually in the *Journal of Asian Studies*. There is no monograph on the civil service as a whole, but aspects of its operation are discussed in a number of interesting recent articles: C. K. Yang, "Some Characteristics of Chinese Bureaucratic Behaviour," in Arthur F. Wright, ed., *Confucianism in Action* (Stanford, 1961), Lawrence J. R. Herson, "China's Imperial Bureaucracy: Its Direction and Control," *Public Affairs Review*, Vol. XVII (1957), pp. 44–53, and John C. Pelzel, "Notes on the Chinese Bureaucracy," *Proceedings of the 1958 Annual Spring Meeting of the American Ethnological Society*, pp. 50–57. Useful insights into the ethical code by which bureaucracy lived can be gained from James T. C. Liu, "Some Classifications of Bureaucrats in Chinese Historiography," *Confucianism in Action*, pp. 165–181, and in David S. Nivison, "Ho-shen and His Accusers: Ideology and Political Behaviour in the Eighteenth Century," *Confucianism in Action*, pp. 209–243.

The political context in which problems of civil service recruitment and reform have been discussed is suggested in a number of studies: For the Sung, in James T. C. Liu, "An Early Sung Reformer: Fan Chung-yen," in John K. Fairbank, ed., *Chinese Thought and Institutions* (Chicago, 1957), pp. 105–31, and also in Professor Liu's *Reform in Sung China* (Cambridge, 1959). See also a companion volume in this series, John Meskill, ed., *Wang An-shih: Practical Reformer?* (Boston, 1963). For the Ming, in Charles O. Hucker, "The Tung-lin Movement of the Late Ming Period," *Chinese Thought and Institutions*, pp. 132–162; for the Ch'ing, in W. T. deBary, "Chinese Despotism and the Confucian Ideal: A Seventeenth-Century View," *Chinese Thought and Institutions*, pp. 163–203, as well as in Mary C. Wright, *The Last Stand of Chinese Conservatism* (Stanford, 1957), esp. ch. v.

Chinese source material in translation is sparse. The civil service and the examination system of the T'ang have been dealt with in Robert des Rotours, *Le Traité des Examens, Traduit de la Nouvelle Histoire des T'ang* (Paris, 1932), and in *Traités des Fonctionnaires et de l'Armée, Traduits de la Nouvelle Histoire des T'ang* (Leiden 1947). In an appendix to the former work, des Rotours has translated the *chin-shih* examination papers of one of the most illustrious of T'ang graduates, the poet and official Po Chü-i. The text of the examination questions and essay is also discussed in Arthur Waley, *The Life and Times of Po Chü-i* (London, 1949). One of the much decried eight-legged essays of the later examination system is reproduced in translation in Victor Purcell, *Problems of Chinese Education* (London, 1936).

Much insight into the life of the aspirant and holder of office can be gained from E-tu Zen Sun's *Ch'ing Administrative Terms: A Translation of the Terminology of the Six Boards* (Cambridge, 1961), with its sets of "waiting lists" for aspirant officials which have a very modern ring, and with over 130 entries describing the different derelictions of duty possible in an official career. Reflecting Po Chü-i's subsequent career, we have Eugene Feifel, trans., *Po Chü-i as Censor: His Memorials Presented to Emperor Hsien-tsung during the Years 808–810* (The Hague, 1961). An interesting manual from the eighteenth century, "Precepts for Local Administrative Officials," is translated in part in Sybille van der Sprenkel, *Legal Institutions in Manchu China: A Sociological Analysis* (London, 1962). Officialdom and the examination system have also been treated in Chinese fiction, most unkindly in Wu Ching-tzu's eighteenth-century satire, *The Scholars* (Peking, 1957), which is easily available in this country.

There exist numerous studies of the social backgrounds and behavior of groups of officialdom in various dynasties. Some of them had to be reluctantly excluded from this collection because of space considerations. They supplement the discussion carried on between the covers of this book, and are listed here in chronological order, by dynasties: L. S. Yang, "Great Families of Eastern Han," in E-tu Zen Sun and John deFrancis, *Chinese Social History* (Washington, 1956), pp. 103–134. Professor H. G. Creel of the University of Chicago has read a paper on civil service recruitment in the Han at a meeting of the Association of Asian Studies but has, to my knowledge, not published in this field yet. On pre-T'ang, there is W. Eberhard, *Das Toba-Reich Nordchinas* (Leiden, 1949). On the T'ang, Donald Holzman, "Les débuts du système médiéval de choix et de classement des fonctionnaires: les neuf catégories de l'impartial et juste," Mélanges de l'Institut des Hautes Études Chinoises (Paris, 1957). For the five dynasties period, there is W. Eberhard, *Conquerors and Rulers* (Leiden, 1952). On Sung and post-Sung dynasties, there is Karl A. Wittfogel, *New Light on Chinese Society* (New York, 1938), and *History of Chinese Society: Liao* (Philadelphia, 1949), as well as the fuller works from

which his two articles above have been excerpted. James B. Parsons, "A Preliminary Analysis of the Ming Dynasty Bureaucracy," *Occasional Papers of the Kansai Asiatic Society* (Kyoto, 1959), Vol. VI, pp. 1–16. O. B. Van der Sprenkel, "High Officials in the Ming," *Bulletin of the School of Oriental and African Studies*, Vol. XIV, (1952), pp. 87–114. Professor Van der Sprenkel's more recent "The Geographic Background of the Ming Civil Service," *Journal of the Economic and Social History of the Orient*, Vol. IV (1961), pp. 302–336, presents answers to several problems raised in this volume, particularly by Professors P'an and Fei, and in Professor Kracke's study of regional quotas. Professor Ho's findings on the Ming and Ch'ing civil service are set forth at greater length in his "Aspects of Social Mobility in China, 1368–1911," *Comparative Studies in Society and History*, Vol. I (1959), pp. 330–359, which had a sequel in Vernon K. Dibble and Ho Ping-ti, "The Comparative Study of Social Mobility," *Ibid.*, Vol. III (1961), pp. 315–327, and in a book-length study by Professor Ho, *The Ladder of Success in Imperial China* (New York, 1962). The pioneer study is by Étienne Zi, "Pratique des Examens Littéraires (Shanghai, 1894). Ch'ing mobility has recently been given close attention by Robert Marsh in his book-length study, *The Mandarins: Circulation of Elites in China, 1600–1900* (Glencoe, Ill., 1961). Wolfgang Franke's *The Reform and Abolition of the Traditional Chinese Examination System* (Cambridge, 1960) has a very useful introductory chapter on the history of recruitment processes and on critiques of the examination system. A useful general discussion of mobility is also in Derk Bodde, *China's Cultural Tradition: What and Whither* (New York, 1957), where the major contrasting viewpoints are discussed.

Unfortunately, Western scholars have as yet done little work on the so-called "subbureaucracy" and its relation with the civil service proper; a recent study by Ch'ü

T'ung-tsu, *Local Government in China under the Ch'ing* (Cambridge, 1962), is beginning to fill this gap for the Manchu period.

The debate about the social stratification of traditional China has revolved around the question of the "gentry" and its role in Chinese society. The more important positions have been staked out by W. Eberhard in his *Das Toba-Reich* and restated in *Conquerors and Rulers;* by Chang Chung-li in his *The Chinese Gentry* (Seattle, 1955) and *The Income of the Chinese Gentry* (Seattle, 1962). Like Professor Chang, and unlike Professor Eberhard, Karl A. Wittfogel believes that access to office, not control over property, is the mark of the Chinese elite. He has presented his views most recently in *Oriental Despotism* (New Haven, 1957). Among our other contributors, Fei Hsiao-t'ung has joined the debate on social stratification with his "Peasantry and Gentry," *American Journal of Sociology,* Vol. LII (1946), pp. 1–17, as has, indirectly, E. A. Kracke, Jr. in his "Sung Society: Change within Tradition," *Far Eastern Quarterly,* Vol. XIV (1954/55), pp. 479–488. Traditional Chinese views on social stratification have been illuminated by T. T. Ch'ü in "Chinese Class Structure and Its Ideology," *Chinese Thought and Institutions,* pp. 235–50. Meanwhile, the debate tends to be beclouded by the untenable use of the word "feudal" for post-Han society on the part of all Marxist scholars.

To get a more rounded picture of mobility, there are studies of family and clan institutions, as well as public educational institutions which, by furthering education, advanced mobility for their beneficiaries. The role of the clan in supporting its members' education is discussed, and the limits of clan action are documented in D. Twitchett, "The Fan Clan's Charitable Estate, 1050–1760," *Confucianism in Action,* pp. 97–133. Public education is discussed by Édouard Biot, *Essai sur l'Histoire de l'Instruction Publique en Chine et de la Corporation des Lettrés depuis les Anciens Temps Jusqu'à Nos Jours* (Paris, 1847). More recent is Henry S. Galt, *History of Chinese Educational Institutions:* Vol. I, *To the Five Dynasties* (London, 1951). Much confusion still exists concerning the function of schools, which is somewhat relieved by T. Grimm's recent *Erziehung und Staat im konfuzianischen China der Ming-Zeit* (Hamburg, 1960). The possible influence of maternal relatives on mobility has not been studied systematically. But see L. C. Goodrich, "Maternal Influence: a Note," *Harvard Journal of Asiatic Studies,* Vol. XII (1949), pp. 226–230.

The damaging effects of political "indoctrination" and the intelligentsia's enforced "examination life" have been commented on by Professor Wittfogel in his *Oriental Despotism* and by Professor Chang in *The Chinese Gentry.* More recently scholars have begun to doubt that the rigorous course of Confucian studies either stultified Chinese intellectuals or deprived them of intellectual independence. For such doubts, directly or indirectly expressed, see S. N. Eisenstadt, "The Study of Oriental Despotisms as Systems of Total Power," *Journal of Asian Studies,* Vol. XVII (1957/58), pp. 435–446 (a review of *Oriental Despotism*), and Frederick Mote, "Confucian Eremitism in the Yüan Period," in David S. Nivison and Arthur F. Wright, eds., *The Confucian Persuasion* (Stanford, 1960), pp. 202–240. But the influence of bureaucratic concerns on scholarship and letters has been demonstrated by E. Balazs, "L'histoire comme guide de la pratique bureaucratique," in W. G. Beasley and E. G. Pulleyblank, eds., *Historians of China and Japan* (London, 1961). The great importance of political themes and the concerns of the scholar-official in Chinese literature are too well known to need elaboration. Finally, the educational and moral ideas that shaped officialdom's views of the "man of talent" may be gathered from David Nivison's "The Problem of 'Knowledge' and 'Action' in Chinese Thought since Wang Yang-ming," *Studies in Chinese Thought*, Arthur F. Wright, ed. (Chicago, 1953), pp. 112–145; and Joseph R. Levenson, "The Amateur Ideal in Ming and Early Ch'ing Society: Evidence from Painting," in *Confucian China and Its Modern Fate: The Problem of Intellectual Continuity* (London, 1958).

3 4 5 6 7 8 9 0